Landscapes of
SAMOS

a countryside guide

Fourth edition

Brian and Eileen Anderson

SUNFLOWER BOOKS

For our Mums and Dads

Fourth edition 2002
reprinted with
STOP PRESS 2003

Copyright © 2002, 2003
Sunflower Books™
12 Kendrick Mews
London SW7 3HG, UK
All rights reserved. No
part of this publication
may be reproduced,
stored in a retrieval
system, or transmitted by
any form or by any means,
electronic, mechanical,
photocopying, recording
or otherwise, without the
prior written permission
of the publishers.
Sunflower Books and
'Landscapes' are
Registered Trademarks.

ISBN 1-85691-187-X

Orchis anatolica

Important note to the reader

We hope those who use this book — especially walkers — will take along a good supply of common sense when they explore. Before setting out, *please read the STOP PRESS on pages 135-136;* there have been significant changes to the landscape since this edition was researched in 2001. These changes are not directly due to the massive fires at the end of 2000 (after which we rechecked all the routes), but to further environmental destruction. Read, too, the notes on pages 35 to 44, and the introductory comments at the beginning of each tour and walk (regarding road conditions, equipment, grade, distances and time, etc). Remember that *storm damage, forest fires or bulldozing may make a route unsafe at any time*. If the route is not as we outline it here, and your way ahead is not secure, return to the point of departure. *Never attempt to complete a tour or walk under hazardous conditions!*

It will be very helpful for us to receive your comments (sent in care of the publishers, please) to alert us to further areas that need rechecking prior to publication of the next fully revised edition.

Cover photograph: Ag. Rafael (Alternative walk 3-3)
Title page: above Koumeika (Walk 15)
Photographs: Brian Anderson
Maps: John Underwood
Drawings: Sharon Rochford (pages 79 and 92); all other drawings: Frances Winder
A CIP catalogue record for this book is available from the British Library.
Printed and bound in the UK by J H Haynes & Co Ltd

10 9 8 7 6 5 4 3 2 1

● Contents

4   Landscapes of Samos

Preface

The very mention of a Greek island is enough to conjure up visions of azure blue seas, wave-lapped golden beaches and whitewashed houses, all languorously bathed in endless sunshine. If these are your dreams then you will find this face of Samos so enchanting that you may not even think of looking further. But beyond the beaches lies a verdant island with landscapes of unimagined beauty quietly awaiting discovery. Discover it how you will — by car if you like, or on foot.

Roaming the countryside is without doubt the best way to see the island and to meet the people. No matter what grade of walker you are, whether your pleasure is a short stroll or a stiff, day-long hike in the mountains, there is more than enough scope on the island, and in this book, to keep you happy throughout a holiday or two! And, to make sure you don't waste a single moment of those all-too-precious holidays, why don't you settle back into a comfortable chair and start your planning right now! Sit back while we preview the possibilities, then you can read the details later, before making your choice.

First, stretch your legs and try some of the gentle walks with us. Let's head along a coastal path to two almost inaccessible bays, Mikro and Megalo Seitani — so natural and innocent that you are left with the fervent hope that they remain forever untouched. Enjoy your swim before moving on into the meadows which, in spring, are alive with pink- and purple-hued anemones, or splashed red with a profusion of poppies. Wild flowers abound on Samos, and none gives us more pleasure than the wild orchids which sometimes share our footpath (36 different species has so far been our tally while out walking). Green takes over as we head into the beautiful Valley of the Nightingales. In this softly-cloaked and wooded valley, ivy climbs to the top of the highest trees, rivers flow, and the nightingales really do sing. You might wonder if you have wandered into a different clime!

Head next for the mountains, where yet another face of Samos is to be found, and you need to be no more

5

than a fit rambler to enjoy the Ambelos range to the full. Limestone landscapes hide a treasure of different flowers, like the snowdrops of early spring or the lovely yellow fritillary — only found here. Mountain peaks have their treasures, too — almost forgotten hill forts from a dark age long since past, when the people were driven from their homes and left the island. A hardy few took refuge in these secret and inaccessible places. The giant Kerkis range, stark and impelling, which stands sentinel over the western end of the island, offers a challenge to even the hardiest of walkers. Our route takes you up all the way from sea level to the very highest peak at 1440m/4725ft; not only is it the highest on the island, but the highest in the Aegean.

Amidst all the colour and charm of the island, and inseparable from it, are the people. A warmth and hospitality hardly suspected in the hustle and bustle of the towns is found in plenty in the unhurried life of the countryside. A cheery greeting is often all that is needed and, if you are prepared to try out your Greek, then the response can sometimes be overwhelming. Make sure you have time to drink the ouzo, or eat the beans, the grapes or whatever they press upon you. This is the stuff of which holiday memories are made!

However you choose to see Samos, whether by car or by long or short walks, or simply by visiting some of the picnic spots, our wish is that with the help of this book you will enjoy visiting Samos as much as we do.

Acknowledgements

During our all-too-short visits to Samos we have made many friends, all of whom contributed to the success of our fieldwork. We wish to acknowledge especially the help of the late Stergos Horiatopoulos of Samos Travel and Tourist Agency, for sharing a lifetime's knowledge of the island and directing our feet to the best of the walking (a role now taken up by his daughter, Rena Horiatopoulos-Heath, who continues to offer tremendous support to us and other 'Landscapers'); Triandafilos Panagiotelis (Ross), without whose help we would never have found the old hill forts near Vourliotes; and Transhire (0870 7898000) for support with car hire. To these and all our other friends we say simply, 'thank you'!

Recommended books

A Huxley and W Taylor, *Flowers of Greece*
P and I Davies, with A Huxley, *Wild Orchids of Britain and Europe*

Getting about

The independence and flexibility gained from a **hired car** makes it a popular form of transport. **Taxis** are economical, particularly if you can share the cost, but they are strictly limited by law to carry no more than four passengers. There are different tariffs for day and night, collection from airports, ports, etc, and a small charge per item for luggage. Prices should be displayed. Local journeys are normally metered (you should insist on this) and subject to a minimum charge, but for longer, unmetered journeys, it is important to establish a price before you set out, to avoid the possibility of being overcharged. There is generally not much scope for bargaining on long journey fares, but it does pay to ask around first to establish a norm. Taxi services are concentrated around the towns so, if you are visiting a remote area, do make sure that the taxi will come to collect you at an appointed time. If you have cause for complaint about taxis, report any incident to the tourist police (171), quoting the taxi number.

For many, **coach tours** offer the most comfortable and enjoyable way to see the island.

The **local bus** is the cheapest and most practical way of getting about and, due to the helpfulness of the bus conductors, it soon became our favourite mode of transport when we first visited the island many years ago to research this book. As you can imagine, we used the service so frequently that we eventually became well known to the conductors and drivers alike, and it was not unusual to get a cheery wave as they passed us out walking, or even for them to stop the bus for a quick handshake! What may surprise you, too, is the efficiency and reliability of the service: it is always best to arrive early, to be sure of catching the bus. All the walks in this book (except Walk 21 and Walk 16 outside high season) can be reached by local bus. Complete summer and winter timetables for all the island's buses are given on pages 128-132. There are more hints on using the local bus service on page 128.

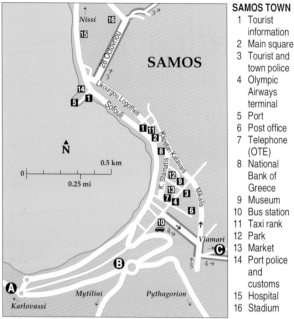

SAMOS TOWN
1 Tourist information
2 Main square
3 Tourist and town police
4 Olympic Airways terminal
5 Port
6 Post office
7 Telephone (OTE)
8 National Bank of Greece
9 Museum
10 Bus station
11 Taxi rank
12 Park
13 Market
14 Port police and customs
15 Hospital
16 Stadium

KARLOVASSI
1 Tourist information
2 Main square
3 Port
4 Post office
5 Telephone (OTE)
6 National Bank of Greece
7 Bus station
8 Taxi rank
9 Port police and customs
10 Stadium
11 Hospital

❀ Picnicking

There are many pretty and varied places to picnic on Samos. The island's official picnic sites are heavily wooded and provide tables and children's play areas. For most of the year they are very quiet, but this changes during the summer months, when the islanders come out to play and picnic (which they love). The shade these sites provide is then much sought after.

For those of you who prefer a more unspoilt, secluded location, try some of the picnic spots along the routes of our walks. We have endeavoured to give you a wide-ranging choice.

All the information you need to get to these picnics is given on the following pages, *where picnic numbers correspond to walk numbers.* (The picnic suggestion prefixed 'CT' is specifically linked to Car tour 3.) You can quickly find the general location on the island by looking at the fold-out touring map inside the back cover, where the walks are outlined in green. We include transport details (🚐: how to get there by bus; 🚗: where to leave your private transport), how long a walk you'll have, and views or setting. Beside the picnic title you'll find a map reference: the exact location of the picnic spot is shown on this *walking* map by the symbol *P* printed in green; 🚐 and 🚗 symbols indicate the nearest access by bus or private transport. Finally, to help you choose a setting that appeals to you, many of the picnic spots are illustrated.

Please remember that if more than a few minutes' walking is required, you should wear sensible shoes and take a sunhat (○ indicates a picnic in full sun).

If you are travelling to your picnic by bus, refer to the timetables on pages 128-132, but remember it's always a good idea to get up-to-date timetables from the bus station as soon as you arrive on the island.

If you are travelling to your picnic by hired transport, be extra vigilant off the main roads: children and animals are often in the village streets. Be careful where you park: don't damage the vegetation and flowers, and be sure not to block a road or track.

All picnickers should read the Country code on page 44 and go quietly in the countryside.

Picnic food suggestions

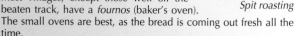

It isn't always easy in a strange country to know what to take on a picnic, so here are a few ideas. Buy your bread fresh each day; most villages, except those well off the beaten track, have a *fournos* (baker's oven).

Spit roasting

The small ovens are best, as the bread is coming out fresh all the time.

From the local market buy fresh *angouri* (cucumber), *domates* (tomatoes), *marouli* (lettuce), *feta* (goat's milk cheese; this is best bought directly from the tub where it is stored covered in brine, since it becomes strongly flavoured and dry when left uncovered). There is also a good selection of cooked sausages and meat available in the supermarkets. Don't forget some olives (the variety on Samos is especially good) and the Greek specialities *tzatziki* and *taramo-salata*. Fruit in season is another good choice.

You can also buy take-away food from tavernas; good choices here are *kotopoulo* (spit-roasted chicken), *souvlaki* (veal on a skewer), and *horiatiki* (Greek salad). Buy the night before if you have a fridge, otherwise ask the taverna owner to keep them in the fridge for you until the morning, and arrange a time to collect them.

Last but not least, don't forget something to drink. Besides mineral water there is the commonly-seen *Samaina sec* wine (not to be confused with the famous sweet muscat wine; see page 14). On Samos it is possible to take an empty container and buy wine, retsina, ouzo and brandy straight from the barrel, sold by weight. It's much cheaper too!

1 PROFITIS ILIAS, KAMBOS (map on reverse of touring map) ○

by car or taxi: 15-25min on foot   by bus: 6-8min on foot
🚗 Park at Kambos, in the lay-by opposite the Vourliotes road junction (the road is too narrow to park closer). Walk west along the old coast road for about 1km, then follow Walk 1, page 40.
🚌 Samos-Karlovassi bus to the Paleohori/Svalas Beach road junction (Timetables 1, 1 A). Follow Walk 1, page 40.
Views over the plain to the sea; backdrop of steeply-terraced hillsides. The church (interesting frescoes) is surrounded by wild flowers in spring.

2a OLEANDER VALLEY near Vourliotes (map on reverse of touring map)

by car or taxi: 15-40min on foot   by bus: not easily accessible
🚗 Park at entrance to Vourliotes and walk back downhill for 0.8km, or park by the concrete road off to the left, about 4.4km uphill from the Vourliotes junction; this concrete road leads to the trail down to the picnic spot — refer to the map on reverse of touring map.
Pleasant spot by a stream, in a quiet valley.

2b AG. KONSTANTINOS (map on reverse of touring map; photograph page 51)

by car or taxi: no walking   by bus: no walking
🚗 Park by the picnic spot on the coast road at the edge of the village.
🚌 Samos-Karlovassi bus to the Ano Ag. Konstantinos junction (Timetables 1, 1A). The picnic spot is by the bus stop.
Ample shade; sea views; picnic tables; children's play area.

3a STONE SHELTER (map pages 56-57, nearby photo pages 54-55)

20-30min on foot from the stadium in Samos town
Use the notes for the start of Walk 3, page 55.
*Picnic on a shaded terrace with lovely views out over Samos town
and beyond. A peaceful setting on the edge of a pine wood.*

3b PROFITIS ILIAS near Samos town (map pages 56-57) ○

1h on foot from the stadium in Samos town
Use notes for the start of Walk 3, page 55.
*Panoramic views of Samos Bay and the eastern side of the island.
The only shade is provided by the walls of the church, but this setting
is well worth the 400m/1300ft climb.*

4 ZOODOCHOU PIGIS (map pages 56-57, photographs pages 28 and 61) ○

by car or taxi: no walking   *by bus: not easily accessible*
🚗 Park at Zoodochou Pigis.
*Seating is provided, but there is little shade. Commanding views out
over the eastern tip of Samos, across to Turkey. You could walk from
here back downhill to Samos town in about 2h15min, using the
notes and map for Walk 4 from the 1h31min-point (page 61).*

5 PSILI AMMOS (map page 65, nearby photograph page 63) ○

by car or taxi: up to 30min on foot   *by bus: 5-10min on foot*
🚗 Park by roadside in Psili Ammos (no walking); in summer it is very
busy here; you may have to park further away (up to 30min on foot).
🚌 Bus to Psili Ammos (summer only; Timetable 5).

A stroll round the back of Samos town

*This pleasant stroll (5km/3mi) can easily fill half a day. You can cut
it short at any number of points, as indicated below.*
Follow Walk 3 (page 56) as far as the 19min-point. Turn right, and
follow this track along the contours of the hill behind Samos town;
the route is marked with orange dots on the map on pages 56-57.
*(The concrete track down to the right, soon reached, leads back into
town.)* When you meet the Vlamari road on a bend, keep straight
ahead. Stay ahead at the next bend, too, on a minor track which
becomes a path. Follow this downhill to a cobbled trail (the 15min-
point in Walk 4) and turn left uphill. When you meet the road at the
top of the trail, keep ahead, then soon turn right on the concrete
road signposted to Vathy. At the point where this road starts to
descend, fork sharply down to the right on an old trail signposted
Ag. Ioannis Thermaston (or stay on the road). Follow this trail down
to the church. The onward route continues up the trail ahead. *(But
a right turn here would take you back to Samos town to the 5min-
point in Walk 4.)* The trail (which cuts off a long loop in the road)
rises to meet the road on a bend. Keep ahead; you soon reach the
theatre in Vathy ('Ti Giannaki'); below it is an old Byzantine church.
Continue into Vathy by forking right just past the theatre. *(The fork
to the left leads round the top of the village and meets the trail
coming down from Paleokastron at around the 2h39min-point in
Walk 5.)* If you've followed us all the way into the centre of Vathy,
you'll come to Captain Likourgis Platea: from here head right
downhill, to return to Samos town.

Samos is an island of flowers, with none more eye-catching than the poppy — the flower of the goddess Aphrodite.

Beautiful sandy beach, umbrellas, tavernas. Close proximity to Turkey, just across the water. If the beach is too crowded, wander towards Pythagorion, to see the flamingo lake.

6a SHADED OASIS (map page 67)

by car or taxi: no walking   *by bus: not easily accessible*

🚗 Travelling from the direction of Samos town via Mytilini, turn left to Ag. Triades about 1km beyond Mytilini. Just before the road bends left to Moni Ag. Triades, turn right along a motorable track (due to be surfaced). In around three minutes, at the head of the valley, keep ahead: the oasis is a further 300m/yds ahead, on the left.

Located at the head of a valley, with views out over the sea to Turkey. You can also enjoy a good view of the ancient wall on Mount Kastri.

6b MOUNT KASTRI (map page 67) ○

by car or taxi: 20min on foot   *by bus: 50min-1h10min on foot*

🚗 Park at Moni Spilianis (see 6c below).

🚌 Bus from Samos to Pythagorion (Timetables 2, 4, 4A) and walk to Moni Spilianis (see map page 67).

Follow the waymarked path from the monastery to Mount Kastri, from where there are excellent views over Pythagorion.

6c MONI SPILIANIS (map page 67)

by car or taxi: no walking   *by bus: 40-50min on foot*

🚗 Park at the monastery: turn right off the Mesokambos-Pythagorion road as you enter Pythagorion (signposted for the Evpalinus Tunnel).

🚌 Bus from Samos to Pythagorion (Timetables 2, 4, 4A); walk to Moni Spilianis (see map page 67).

Lovely shaded terrace inside the monastery, with picnic tables. Overlooking Pythagorion. Don't forget to visit the chapel in the cave.

7 VALLEY OF THE NIGHTINGALES (map on reverse of touring map, nearby photograph page 25)

by car or taxi: 2min on foot   *by bus: 14min on foot*
🚗 Park by the side of the road above Platanakia (at Platanakia, turn south up the road to Manolates). After 0.75km descend a well-waymarked path to the left. The picnic spot is beyond the stream.
🚌 Samos-Karlovassi bus to Platanakia (Timetables 1,1A). Walk up the Manolates road (opposite where the bus stops) for about 12min, then turn left down the well-waymarked path.
A flower-filled meadow in springtime, surrounded by trees and with a stream running alongside. The stream is shown on page 25.

14 PETALOUDES (map page 97, photograph page 95)

by car or taxi: 25-35min on foot   *by bus: not easily accessible*
🚗 Park on outskirts of Ydroussa and follow Walk 14 from the 1h52min-point, to leave Ydroussa on the street called Odos Kapetan Laxana.
A lovely glade with views over to the Kerkis mountains.

Island flora
All the elements favouring diverse plant growth come together with striking effect on Samos. Its island character ensures mild winters; plenty of high ground and the proximity of the Turkish mountains ensure a good winter rainfall. Limestone geology, too, supports a wide range of plants. The island's mountains are not only extensive, but high enough to support a whole range of habitats and provide a cooler climate throughout the year. The result is that Samos has an unusually rich flora.

Spring starts early, but the best months for flowers are March and April. By May it is often necessary to look to the higher ground for the best flowers (unless there has been a late spring). Bulbous plants, which have the opportunity to retire below ground to escape the heat of the summer, are common here as on other Greek islands. Blue muscari is everywhere in March and April, but special to Samos is the yellow, sweetly-scented *Muscari macrocarpum*. Orchids, too, abound, but they often blend so well into their surroundings that they are overlooked by many walkers. Anemones, poppies, the white daisy, *Anthemis chia*, and geraniums are all common, but some of the rarer specialities include the lovely red paeony, *P mascula* (shown here and on page 124), and two yellow fritillaries, *F bithynica* and the hard-to-find *F carica*.

Autumn walkers too can enjoy some flowers. *Cyclamen hederifolium* bursts into bloom quite spectacularly after the first rains, together with a variety of crocus and colchicums. Those who look carefully might just spot a pale blue muscari, *M parviflorum*, as delicate as baby's breath, which is the common name sometimes given to this plant.

Wines of Samos

The grapes for the island's wines are grown largely on the north side of the Ambelos mountains, and it is a special pleasure to do Walks 1 and 2 in September, when the farmers are all busy gathering the harvest. Six commercial wines are on offer. One is the amber-coloured sweet dessert wine often called 'Samos nectar'. Do not confuse this with the island's dry wine, *Samaina sec,* which is sold in small 500g bottles and reasonably priced. The wine usually offered to tourists is the more expensive and superior *Samaina special,* which arrives in standard 750g-size green bottles. Three newer wines especially introduced for the tourist market are *Samena golden* (a dry white), *Selano* (rosé) and *Doryssa* (a fruity dry white).

If you enjoy *retsina,* the resinated wines mostly consumed by the Greeks themselves, ask for *'spitiko krasi'* (house wine) and hope for the best. Some of it is poor quality, but equally some is excellent, far better than most of the commercial varieties ... so it is worth the risk.

17a AG. TRIADA above Karlovassi (town plan page 8) ○

| by car or taxi: 15min on foot | by bus: not easily accessible |

🚗 Park by the port in Karlovassi and walk up the narrow surfaced road opposite the port. Look for an old trail up left, as the road bends to the right. On reaching Paleo Karlovassi, turn left and continue up to Ag. Triada.
Excellent vantage point with panoramic views.

17b CHAPEL ON THE POTAMI TRAIL (Karlovassi town plan page 8 and map pages 114-115)

| by car or taxi: 30-40min on foot | by bus: not easily accessible |

🚗 The nearest parking is by the port in Karlovassi. Follow the instructions for Picnic 17a but, instead of turning left for Ag. Triada, turn right. Continue up to the main square. Then use the notes for Walk 17 (page 107) from the 28min-point to reach the chapel.
Very secluded location. Large terrace hidden from the trail, with some shade, and views down over the olive groves to the sea.

17c BYZANTINE CHURCH above Potami (map pages 114-115, photograph page 119)

| by car or taxi: 2-5min on foot | by bus: not easily accessible |

🚗 Park in Potami near the start of the track to the Byzantine church (signposted in English 'to Byzantine church').
Shaded terrace with picnic tables next to the church. Another good picnic spot is at a castle 4min uphill from the church (photograph page 107), but there is little shade. To get there, see notes page 109.

17d RIVER GORGE near Potami (map pages 114-115)

| by car or taxi: 15-20min on foot | by bus: not easily accessible |

🚗 Park as for Picnic 17c; follow notes on page 189 (just after the 1h15min-point) to walk from the Byzantine church to the gorge.
Plenty of shade. Picnic in a pretty glade at the gorge entrance.

18a POTAMI BAY (map pages 114-115) ○

by car or taxi: no walking   *by bus: not easily accessible*
🚗 Park along the coast road, by the beach.
Super, fairly sandy and picturesque bay. Taverna, facilities in season.

18b MIKRO SEITANI (map pages 114-115, photograph page 121) ○

by car or taxi: 40-45min on foot   *by bus: not easily accessible*
by jeep: 25-35min on foot
🚗 Park at end of the surfaced road in Potami. You can continue 1km
further by jeep (on a track). Then start Walk 18 (page 112).
*Wonderful intimate sandy bay — but beware when swimming,
unless it is calm; there is a danger of being scraped against rocks.*

CT3 POSIDONION (refer to car touring map; photograph page 17)

by car or taxi: up to 5min on foot
🚗 Park on the edge of the woods as you enter Posidonion, or near
the seashore.
*Picnic either in shade of the woods or on the stony seashore. There
are tavernas by the sea. Very close to Asia Minor.*

*Samos Bay from above Moni Vronda (Walk 13), with Profitis Ilias
(Walk 3) above Samos town*

❀ Touring

Samos isn't a large island and at present has limited surfaced roads, although the situation is continually improving. Hiring a car is useful if you want to see a good selection of the island's landscapes. With this in mind we have put together three car touring itineraries and have included a jeep 'safari' for more intrepid explorers.

Car hire charges are moderate, with a higher rate for jeeps. Beware when renting: many of the cars, and particularly the motorbikes, are not serviced regularly, and breakdowns are not uncommon. Before setting out, check the car and clarify the rental conditions/ insurance coverage. Motorists are strongly advised to make sure that they have 'collision damage waiver' insurance cover, and not just standard third party cover. They are liable for any damage to their *own* hired car under third party insurance and could find themselves in jail until the repair costs are forthcoming. Always carry the agency's telephone number with you, and take some water, food and warm clothing in case of breakdown.

The touring notes are brief: they include little history or information about towns: all this is freely available from the tourist offices. Instead, we concentrate on the 'logistics' of touring: times and distances, road conditions, viewpoints, and good places to rest. Most of all, we emphasise possibilities for **walking** and **picnicking**. (The symbol *P* is used to alert you to a picnic spot: see pages 9-15.) We've also highlighted some circular walks (labelled 'CW') for motorists, of less than two hours' walking time.

The tours start in Samos town, but you can join them easily if you are staying at one of the other main resorts. If you only hire a car for one day, try Tour 1, which will give you a good preview of the island's landscapes.

The large touring map is designed to be held out opposite the touring notes and contains all the infor mation you will need outside Samos town. **Allow plenty of time for stops:** our times include only short breaks at viewpoints labelled (📷). Note that **petrol stations** are often closed on Sundays, except in the main towns, where you'll usually find one open. Card-operated **telephones** are located near post offices, by the telephone exchange (OTE), and at some kiosks. A card is useful for calls home and also for walkers who require a taxi (particularly out of season). Hotels, tavernas, cafés and shops will let you use their phones at the local rate. **Public toilets** are available in the larger towns; others are found in bars and cafés. Don't rely on toilet paper being available; carry your own.

Distances quoted are cumulative kilometres from Samos town. The key to the symbols in the notes is on the touring map.

All motorists should read the Country code on page 44 and go quietly in the countryside.

Posidonion, with views across to Asia Minor (Picnic CT3)

1 ROUND THE ISLAND

Samos town • Manolates • Karlovassi • Maratho-kambos • Votsalakia • Pyrgos • Koumaradei • Chora • Mytilini • Samos town

126km/78mi; about 4 hours' driving; Exit A from Samos town

On route: Picnics (see pages 9-15) (1), 2b, (6a), 7, 17a-b, (17c-d, 18a-b); Walks 1, 2, 6-9, (10), 11, 12, (13, 14), 17, (18), 19, (20), 21; Circular walks (CW) 1, (2, 3), 4, (5), 7, 8

The road from Samos town to Karlovassi is good. Petrol is available in Samos town, Kokkari and Karlovassi.

The sights of Samos lie not in the abundance of popular ancient ruins, but in the variety and flavour of its ever-changing landscape. If you only have a car for a day, then this tour will give you a sample of as much of its beauty as possible. You will see lush green valleys reminiscent of a more temperate climate and towering mountains, some verdantly clad, others stark and impelling. Pine forests will shade your way, and the clear turquoise sea will beckon enticingly. Sleepy villages, basking in the sun, are waiting for you to stop and stretch your legs. How will you be able to resist exploring this wonderland on foot?

Leave Samos town along the coast road to Karlovassi (Exit A). For this tour we suggest you drive without stopping through **Kokkari** (11km ✝🏔🛖✕🚮⊕). It is a picturesque spot and definitely worth a visit, but it is easily accessible by bus. However, if you're ready to stretch your legs, try the circular walk below: park about 1km further on, just as you leave the village.

Continue along the coast road through **Avlakia** (✕) to pass the Vourliotes junction (17.5km). Less than 1km later, the narrow concrete trail up left (**P**1) is the start of Walk 1 and heads up to Vourliotes by an old route.

Platanakia (20.4km ✕) is reached as you turn inland again and cross a bridge, after which you turn left up

🚗 Circular walk (CW) suggestion

CW1: 4.5km/2.8mi; 1h; easy. This is a gentle walk that quickly gets you into the countryside behind **Kokkari.** Start by following the narrow road at the end of the bypass, 1km west of Kokkari. As it reverts to concrete track, keep left at the next junction. Stay on the main track as it winds uphill and then eastwards, back behind Kokkari. In 25min you reach a path off to the left. Now you have joined the final section of Walk 8. Use the notes from the 1h31 min-point in that walk (page 76) to return to the centre of Kokkari. From there turn left and follow the coast road for 12min to return to the starting point and your car. **Map on reverse of touring map.**

the lush green **Valley of the Nightingales** (photograph page 25; near *P*7), towards Manolates. Just under 1 km up this road, on your left, is the setting for Picnic 7 and, if you feel like walking up to Manolates (Circular walk 4, see page 24), park just beyond the taverna on your right, after about 1.6km. As you clear the woodland, enthuse over the views (🎦) of awe-inspiring vineyard terraces. Walks 2 and 12 pass through sleepy **Manolates** (24.2km ✝✕🎦; photographs pages 4 and 87) perched on the mountainside. Park at the entrance to the village or in the car park further uphill. There are plenty of tavernas and an interesting fountain near the top of the village.

When you can tear yourself away from this tranquil spot, return to Platanakia and turn left towards Karlovassi. Two minutes later you reach **Ag. Konstantinos** (▲✕🚡*P*2b). Walk 2 ends here, near the church shown in the photograph on page 51. The road hugs the coast almost all the way to **Karlovassi** (41.4km ✝▲▲▲✕ 🚊⊕WC; *P*17a-b), the starting point for Walks 17 and 19. Circular walk 8 (page 31) also begins here, at the port. If you have time, you can make a quick trip to Potami Bay (*P*17c-d, 18a-b); see Car tour 2, page 25. It's the starting point for Walks 18 and 20, as well as Circular walk 5, described on page 24.

Otherwise, continue on the road ahead and keep left when it reaches the river bed. To go into Neo Karlovassi, take the next left turn, up the road opposite the bridge (just after turning alongside the river bed), but keep straight on for Marathokambos. Although Karlovassi isn't a very attractive town, our walks take you into magnificent countryside within a surprisingly short time.

As you leave Karlovassi behind and head south, the views open up, and you will marvel at the awesome Kerkis range (🎦) across to your right. At **Ag. Theodori** (50.2km) turn sharp right. Your route now takes you through a fire-ravaged pine forest, which is fortunately regenerating, and on to **Marathokambos** (56.6km ✝▲▲▲✕🎦). Walk 21 ends in this village, which sprawls across a hillside. To reach the centre, continue down between the houses until you reach a square, where you can park. Then walk left into the town.

Or continue down the spaghetti-like road towards Ormos Marathokambos, enjoying the seascapes (🎦) as you descend. On reaching the bottom, follow the

main road down to the coast, bypassing Ormos Marathokambos (61.5km) on the way. The beach, gently
lapped by the invitingly-clear turquoise sea, stretches
ahead of you as far as Votsalakia and beyond; choose
your own picnic spot. A backdrop of stark mountains
and undulating hills completes the setting (🎞).

The almost magnetic quality of the impressive Kerkis
range draws you on to **Votsalakia** (**Kambos**; 65.5km
🏠🏠▲✕). It's from here that challenging Walk 16
begins. Can you spot the white monastery, Evangelistria, set amid trees on the side of Kerkis? There's a
close-up photo of it on page 103.

With the mountains behind you, now retrace your
route, enjoying fine views of Marathokambos slum-
bering on the hillside. When you reach **Ag. Theodori**
again (80.8km), turn right towards Pyrgos. The road
undulates and winds around the hillside, passing (after
2km) the road up to Platanos, where Walk 14 starts,
and the right-hand turn-off to Balos. Forest fires have
decimated much of the pine forest in the **Pyrgos** area
(94.3km ▲✕🎞), but it is still worth while stretching
your legs here. Park at the side of the road near the taxi
stand and bus stop, on the edge of the village. The
centre is just across the road, beyond the taverna.

Possible detour (12km): If you were to drive up the
road on your left here (by the taxi stand), you would
come to Pandrosos, which is the starting point for the
circular walk below. You can park at the entrance to
the village at an obvious car park (just past a chapel on
the left, by a narrow concrete road). This car park is
also convenient for Walks 12 and 13.

Wend your way in a leisurely fashion to **Koumaradei**
(99.2km ✕). On arrival, park where the road widens,
a little past the craft shops (which are worth a visit). As
you leave and wind down the road, there is a good
vantage point (🎞) from where you look back at the
village and can appreciate to the full its strategic

🚗 Circular walk (CW) suggestion

CW2: 4.5km/2.8mi; 1h20min; easy-moderate. There is some stiff
climbing from **Pandrosos**, as you follow part of the route up towards
Profitis Ilias (the highest peak in the Ambelos), but the views make
the effort worthwhile. Follow Walk 12 (page 88) as far as the 42min-
point, where the main walk turns right. Instead, turn left to follow
the track back to Pandrosos. **Map on reverse of touring map;
photographs opposite and page 91.**

🚗 Circular walk (CW) suggestion

CW3: 2.4km/1.5mi; 35min; easy. This is Short walk 9 from **Mavratzei** (see page 77). Enjoy a pleasant stroll into the countryside beyond this interesting village. **Map on reverse of touring map.**

position. You are now descending along the hillside in the direction of Chora, with views (📷) down over the plain to Ireon.

Suggested detour (3km): When you have travelled 3.7km from Koumaradei, there is a road off sharp left which leads up to Mavratzei. Walks 9 and 10 and Picnic 9 (see photograph pages 78-79) start off from there, as does the circular walk above. It's well worth the detour, especially for the extensive views on the climb up to the village (📷). You can park on the outskirts of Mavratzei. When you leave, the road continues through the village and back down to the main road, passing the monastery of Timiou Stavrou on the way. Turn left at the main road.

Chora (109.3km ✕ 🏠) is soon reached, where Walk 11 begins. Here you turn left back towards Samos town (past the road off right to Moni Ag. Triades; *P*6a, photograph pages 68-69). Heading north now, with the foot-

Climb up through the narrow village streets at Pandrosos, to the square with this colourful church. Walks 12 and 13 begin here.

Touring hint
Drive carefully; the road is regarded as a pavement, especially in country areas. In towns, take extra care in the one-way systems which tend to be abused, especially at night. During the high season there are also many first-time drivers of mopeds and motorbikes on the road and, as in most parts of Greece, a correspondingly high accident rate. If you do hire a moped or motorbike, crash helmets are mandatory, but life goes on without them ... and they are not supplied by the hire companies. Check your holiday insurance cover.

hills of the Ambelos range to your left and the plain of Mytilini on the right, you pass the Museum of Palae-ontology on the left as you enter **Mytilini** (112.9km ♦✕🖭M). The museum is open daily from 09.00 (10.00 on Sundays) to 14.30. Mytilini is very much a working village and the focal point for several walks: Walks 6-8 begin here, and Walk 9 ends here. Should you want to look around, it's easier to park at either end of the village rather than in the centre

From here it is little more than 13km back to Samos town. There are panoramic views (📷) behind you as you climb up and away from Mytilini, and ahead you look out over Samos Bay (📷), as you descend to end the tour in **Samos town** (126km).

Blue Chairs taverna in Vourliotes (Car tour 2; Walks 1, 2 and 7)

2 THE VERDANT NORTH

**Samos town • Vourliotes • Moni Vronda • Manolates
• Karlovassi • Potami • Leka • Kastania • Karlovassi
• Samos town**

111km/69mi; about 4 hours' driving; Exit A from Samos town

On route: Picnics (see pages 9-15) (1), 2a-b, 7, (14), 17a-d, 18a-b;
Walks 1, 2, 7, 12, 13-3, (14), 17-20; Circular walks (CW) 1, 4-8

*The roads are quite good. Get your petrol in Samos town, Kokkari
or Karlovassi.*

This is an ideal tour to sample the lush northern
shore of Samos. Drink your fill of mountains
standing sentinel over vineyards towering upwards as
far as the eye can see. Enjoy a refreshing swim from
one of the many beaches you pass, lapped by a clear
turquoise sea.

Start this tour as Tour 1 (page 18) but, when you get
to the Vourliotes junction (17.5km), turn left for
Vourliotes and Moni Vronda, two very popular
attractions. You now wind uphill; take care on the
bends, while enjoying views (📷) of the sylvan
landscape all the way up to **Vourliotes** (22.7km ✕).
Walks 1 and 2 pass through here, and Picnic 2a is
nearby. Park either at the entrance to the village or a
short way up the road towards Moni Vronda. Vourliotes is popular because of its traffic-free village
square, the *platea* shown opposite, in the heart of the
village; you reach it by continuing on foot from where
you have parked. The *platea* has a peaceful old-world
atmosphere and is a great place to sit with drink in
hand, watching the world go by. If you feel like a snack,
ask for the special *keftedes;* they're made of chick peas,
and they're delicious. When you're ready, take the
steeply-winding road (signposted) to Moni Vronda,
situated up to your left as you enter Vourliotes.

On reaching **Moni Vronda★** (24.7km ♨🏠📷), the
oldest monastery on the island, leave your car at the
side of the road. It is easy to understand why a
monastery was built here, with its commanding views
down over the north coast and its air of tranquillity.
Walks 1 and 7 and Alternative walk 13-3 pass through
this secluded setting, shown on pages 15 and 45.

From Moni Vronda retrace your route back to the
Vourliotes junction (31.9km), enjoying views (📷) from
different vantage points on your descent. Turn left at
the junction and then head through **Kambos** (*P*1) to
Platanakia (34.8km ✕), where you turn left up the road

23

🚗 Circular walk (CW) suggestion

CW4: 6km/3.75mi; 1h30min; easy-moderate. This circuit involves some climbing, but it shows you the very best of the beautiful **Valley of the Nightingales**. Leave the car 1.6km up the Manolates road and continue along the road on foot, with your back to the sea. You meet a bridge, where the road swings left. Start the walk here, by crossing the bridge and immediately taking the footpath on the left. Follow the waymarks as you climb up through immaculately-maintained terraced vineyards. When the trail ends, turn right to a church. Go left here, and then turn right when you meet a track. In under 3min you will find your continuing trail up to the left. At 25min you finally emerge on the road, where you turn left for Manolates, reaching the centre in 45min. Follow the road to return. **Map on reverse of touring map.**

to Manolates. The **Valley of the Nightingales** (*P*7) is surely one of the most beautiful on Samos. As you drive up this valley, unbelievably green in spring, stop the car and listen for the song of the nightingale. On the left, just under 1 km along, lies the setting for Picnic 7 — the photograph opposite was taken nearby. If you are inclined to take a walk, park after about 1.6km (just beyond a taverna on your right) and use the notes above.

The vista opens up as you approach Manolates. Park at the entrance to the village. Walks 2 and 12 (photographs pages 4 and 87) visit **Manolates** (39.1 km ♥🏨✕ 📷). The village exudes an almost timeless quality as it slumbers on a hillside ledge, but you will enjoy equally the return down the valley back to **Platanakia** (43.4km), where you turn left for Karlovassi (*P*2b at **Ag. Konstantinos**). As you drive along, skimming the coast, the hills will at times appear almost to nudge you into the sea; at other times they will entice your eye to wander further inland, up verdant valleys. Notice the road up to Ydroussa (Walk 14), about 1km before Karlovassi. If you want to visit Petaloudes, the beautiful picnic spot shown on page 95 *(P*14*)*, turn off here.

Entering **Karlovassi** (55.8km ♥🏨▲♦✕🖃⊕WC), the main town is to your left (see Car tour 1, page 19) but, to reach Potami Bay, take a right turn (signposted 'Port'). You are now back by the shore. If Ag. Triada, prominently sited on a hill ahead, intrigues you, then try walking up to it. Park by the port (*P*17a-b) and use the notes for Circular walk 8 on page 31. Otherwise continue on around the headland in front of you, passing a white church in modern style as you reach **Potami**

🚗 Circular walk (CW) suggestion

CW5: 2km/1.25mi; 36min; easy. Park in **Potami** by the track to the Byzantine church (signposted). Use the notes on page 108 (just after the 1h07min-point to walk to the church, the castle and the gorge. Return the same way. **Map pages 114-115.**

Circular walk 4: the Valley of the Nightingales, the beautiful valley that carries the road from Platanakia up to Manolates. Picnic 7 lies lower down this valley.

🚗 Circular walk (CW) suggestion

CW6: 4.4km/2.75mi; 1h; easy. This walk gives you a good sample of the lush vegetation in the shadow of the Kerkis range. Walks 16 and 18-21 penetrate deep into this region. Start the walk at the sharp right turn in **Leka**, along the road signposted for Kastania. When the main road swings left in 2min, keep straight on and look for a track on the left reached 1min after the road surface ends (7min). Now pick up the notes for Walk 19 at the 1h01min-point (page 117) and fork left down the track. Follow these notes to the 1h21min-point. Turn right here and continue downwards alongside a water channel. You reach Tsourlei in 7min. Now turn to page 109 (Walk 17) and use the notes from the 2h16min-point to the 2h36min-point. Keep ahead past the rubbish tip here, back to Leka. **Map pages 114-115.**

Bay (59.8km ✗ 📷 **P**17c-d, 18a-b; photographs pages 107, 119). You will probably be ready to enjoy a refreshing swim and picnic on the beach, but if you feel the urge to explore, try Circular walk 5 on page 24, to climb to the Byzantine church, the castle above it, and the gorge. Walks 18 and 20 also begin here.

Now return to Karlovassi along the shore and pass the port. Turn right (signposted to Samos town) and keep straight ahead to pass a church on the left. Continue as the road swings round to the right, so that you are now facing towards the church on the hill at Paleo Karlovassi. The first narrow road off left leads into Meseo Karlovassi, but you're looking for the second, which winds up to the left, just before a large hotel. Once on the road to Leka you can relax and absorb the scenery around you. On reaching **Leka** (65.8km), watch for the sharp bend in the road in the village centre: if you'd like to try the circular walk above, park tidily either before or after this bend. Walks 17, 19 and 20 pass near the village.

Leaving Leka, you can appreciate the views across the valley (📷) towards Kerkis, and you will have a glimpse of Kastania nestling on the hillside. Your eye will be drawn up the valley, to where the village of Kosmadeo lies hidden. Walk 21 starts in Kosmadeo and leads through some spectacular scenery.

Wooded **Kastania** (70km 📷), which derives its name from the sweet chestnut tree, is entered to the left of an impressive wash-house, situated in a square where you can park. Wander around this still-untouched hillside village, before returning to **Karlovassi** (78.2km) and the coast road back to **Samos town** (111 km).

3 EASTERN HIGHLIGHTS

Samos town • Zoodochou Pigis • Ag. Zoni • Posidonion • Paleokastron • Mykali • Psili Ammos • Mesokambos • Moni Spilianis • Pythagorion • Hera • Ireon • Pagondas • Mili • Chora • Mytilini • Samos town

108km/67mi; 4 hours' driving; Exit C from Samos town

On route: Picnics (see pages 9-15) 4, 5, (6a), 6b-c, CT3; Walks 4-6, (7-9), 11; Circular walk 7

All roads are surfaced.

In complete contrast with Tour 2, this route takes you through more typically arid Mediterranean countryside and includes the important archaeological remains on Samos, about which more information can be found in general tourist literature. Enthuse over the exhilarating views from Zoodochou Pigis and feel the tang of the sea on the beach at Psili Ammos. Cross the plain of Ireon to the site of an ancient wonder, the Temple of Hera, and visit Mili in the heart of orange-growing country. Time will be your enemy, as there is so much to linger over, but take your fill and allow your senses to be invaded by these delights. This is a very full itinerary, so allow for a long day.

Referring to the town plan on page 8, the easiest way to negotiate the maze of narrow streets behind Samos town and find your route, is to take the road up from the promenade, past the bus station. Continue ahead, up a concrete road (which is for one-way traffic). At the end of this road turn right, and you will find yourself in a square dominated by a huge tree. The road you want is to the left now, and signposted for Vlamari.

If you find negotiating hairpin bends thrilling, then this is the route for you. Not that they are particularly difficult... there are just a lot of them. As the road levels out at the top of the hill, keep left at the fork. Continue up the side of the cultivated plain of Vlamari and through the small hamlet of **Kamara** (5.1km ✕), one of the settings for Walk 4. The road ahead, a couple of minutes beyond the village (where the road swings round left) leads down to the beach at Mourtia. You

🚗 Circular walk (CW) suggestion

CW7: 5.1km/3.3mi; 2h; easy to moderate. This good leg-stretcher, with exhilarating views from the church of Profitis Ilias, takes you to one of our favourite picnic spots. The walk starts in **Samos town**. It's Walk 3; see notes on page 54. **Map pages 56-57.**

Blue, representing heaven, caps the dome of the beautiful monastery of Zoodochou Pigis ('the source of life'). The entrance to the monastery is shown in the photograph on page 61.

keep left with the road, winding your way up the side of the hill and marvelling at the vista now opening up before you — the monastery perched just below the summit. **Zoodochou Pigis**★ (8.5km ♦⚲*P*4) at last! Many regard the views to be enjoyed from this vantage point, away over the narrow straits to the mountains of Turkey, as some of the finest on the island.

To reach your next port of call, retrace your route as far as Kamara (13.6km) and turn left to Ag. Zoni. The monastery of **Ag. Zoni** (14.8km) lies tucked away on the left at the end of this road. Nearby is the equally sleepy hamlet of the same name — a short stroll further along the road from the monastery, to the right of the junction. To continue, turn left at the junction beyond the monastery and rise up along a road which skirts the edge of cultivation on the right. In a further 2.5km meet the Paleokastron-Posidonion road and turn left. For the next kilometre, the road passes mainly between cultivated fields, before beginning a spectacular (⚲) downward run to **Posidonion** (25.7km ✕*P*CT3; photograph page 17). Although there isn't much of a beach here, it is pleasant to relax at the water's edge, enjoying a drink in these peaceful surroundings.

Return the same way, past the Ag. Zoni junction, to **Paleokastron** (34.7km ✕). Reach a square on the left and park here, if you wish to explore the village, or follow the road round to the right in the direction of Samos town. At the Psili Ammos junction (35.6km), turn left and follow this road as far as it goes. The flamingo lake (photograph page 63) — one of the highlights of Walk 5 — lies to the left at **Mykali** as you reach the coast. They take up residence in the spring, and remain until the water dries up sometime in the early summer. Recent building by the lake is, however, disturbing the birds, and their numbers are tending to decline. **Psili Ammos** (43.1 km ✕ ☜*P*5) only appears once you have turned inland and skirted the hill now on your right. Park at the roadside. This is the place for a picnic on the beautiful sandy beach or a meal at one of the tavernas ... and a swim in the crystal-clear water.

Retracing your route, take the road off left after 3km, keeping right almost immediately at the next junction. Keep on the road now for a further 3.1 km to where it meets the main Samos-Pythagorion road at **Meso-kambos** (49.2km 🚻; starting point for Walk 5), then turn left towards Pythagorion.

Five kilometres further on, as you are entering Pythagorion, turn up the road on your right signposted to the **Evpalinus Tunnel**★. The tunnel was built by Evpalinus in the Polykrates era, to bring water from the Ambelos mountains. It is 0.5km straight ahead, where the road begins to curl up right to the Spilianis Monastery. Go along this road to see the tunnel and then, on returning to the monastery road junction, turn left. Continue all the way up to **Moni Spilianis**★ (57km ✝☜wc*P*6b-c). Here you can sit on a shaded terrace overlooking Pythagorion. For a closer inspection of the ancient walls (Kastro Polykrati), use the map on page 67 to follow Walk 6 in reverse; this will take you up to them in 15 minutes or less. Don't forget to visit the underground chapel, accessible from inside the

Atmospheric dining

If you like to dine by the quayside, Pythagorion offers the perfect atmosphere, with a good choice of tavernas or restaurants, from the sophisticated to the rustic. Kokkari is another village by the sea that offers perhaps less sophistication but a number of small, interesting tavernas. By way of contrast, many of the smaller villages have tavernas where the tables spill out into the shade of a mighty plane tree. Often these are located in the central *platea* which, in the smaller villages, are free of traffic and are particularly relaxing ... great places to eat, drink and watch the world go by. Mostly the food is simple but, with the soporific atmosphere and the wine, it is fit for the gods. Vourliotes (try the chick-pea *keftedes* at the 'Blue Chairs' taverna), Manolates, and Mili all have small tavernas in such settings.

monastery grounds, before descending again to the main road and turning right into **Pythagorion** (58.4km ✝🛏🏔🔺✗🚐⊕WC), where Walks 6 and 11 end. At the T-junction in Pythagorion you turn right for Ireon, but left to reach the harbour. The harbour is closed to traffic in the summer, so turn right and park in the car park a little further down the road on the left; then walk back, if you fancy a stroll round the harbour.

To continue the tour, follow the signs to Ireon by forking left at the traffic lights, to cross the plain. Just before reaching Ireon, bear left on a small road to the ancient **Temple of Hera★** (66.9km 🏛). A little skilful reconstruction might help to create a better sense of history at this site. To reach Ireon, backtrack to the main road and turn left.

Hera

Ireon (68.4km 🏔🔺✗; photograph page 85) sprawls along the shore. Continue towards Pagondas by taking the wide road on your right, soon after entering the town. This road skirts the plain to the right. You pass **Sarakini's Tower** (🛏) on the right; it was built in 1577 as protection against frequent pirate raids. Turn left on reaching the road up to Pagondas. Once you are clear of the trees and the road straightens out, there are extensive views (📷) across and down the valley to your right. To reach the square in **Pagondas** (76.4km ✝✗) follow the road round to the right, or park on the outskirts and walk.

From Pagondas, return to the T-junction at the bottom of the hill and turn left for **Mili** (81.9km ✝✗). Turn left on reaching the village and park at the roadside a little further along. The traffic-free square, where it is pleasant to sit and have a drink, is then up to your right.

Return in the direction of Pythagorion until you reach the airport (88.9 km), where you go left to **Chora** (90.9km ✗🚐) where Walk 11 starts. It is easy to miss the first turn off to Chora by the airport; if you do, continue for about 0.5km to the major road junction and then turn left, which adds about 1.5km onto your distance at Chora. (If you are pressed for time, you can return to Samos town via Pythagorion by turning right at this junction; it is a faster route than the one we use.)

To return to Samos town, use the notes for Car tour 1 on page 22: this picturesque route takes you past the road to Moni Ag. Triades (**P**6a, photograph pages 68-69) and through **Mytilini** (Walks 6-9).

4 JEEP SAFARI: WESTERN HIGHLIGHTS

Samos town • Karlovassi • Leka • (Kosmadeo) • Kastania • Marathokambos • Votsalakia (Kambos) • Drakei • Balos • Koumeika • Skoureika • Pyrgos • Chora • Mytilini • Samos town

167.5km/104mi; about 8 hours' driving; Exit A from Samos town

On route: Picnics (see pages 9-15) (1), 2b, 17a-b; Walks 1, 2, 6-9, 11, 15-21; Circular walks (CW) 1, 6-8

On this tour you will only encounter a few unsurfaced sections between Ormos Marathokambos and Koumeika and between Kallithea and Drakei. These are the only two lengthy stretches of track, plus any minor diversions you may wish to make off the tourist route, down to the beaches along the Drakei run.

Although there is much to delight the eye touring Samos, a jeep enables you to discover places that are less accessible by car. This tour mostly explores the west of the island, finishing up on the south coast. Once you leave the north, you will find yourself in more typically Mediterranean terrain, cloaked in *phrygana* and *macchie*. There are also many pretty beaches, with a sea just as inviting as it is on the north coast. To get the most out of this tour, do make an early start!

Leave Samos town by Exit A and follow the coast road (see Car tour 1, page 18) straight to **Karlovassi** (32.8km ♣⛰🏠✕🚉⊕WC; *P*17a-b), where the circular walk below starts at the port. Walks 17 and 19 begin and end in the town centre. Fill up with petrol here, as you will be going a long way with little or no chance of finding any.

Finding your onward route to Leka is a little tricky, but see the town plan of Karlovassi on page 8 and follow these notes carefully. On reaching Karlovassi, follow the main road towards Marathokambos; then, shortly after the road turns left alongside the river, turn right over the bridge. The road bends round to the right and then to the left, passing a church on the right. At

🚙 Circular walk (CW) suggestion

CW8: 3.5km/2.2mi; 50min; easy. Use the notes for Picnic 17a (page 14) to climb to Ag. Triada. To return, head down from the church keeping straight on (as if making for the village square) but, after just 1min, look for the cobbled trail going down left. Follow it down and continue to the right as it runs into a track. When you emerge on the road, 15min after leaving the church, turn left to head back to the seafront and left again back to **Karlovassi**'s port. **Map pages 114-115; town plan page 8**.

Village names

At the beginning of the 15th century, Samos was under the protection of the Genoan, Giustiani, whose base was on Chios. When Giustiani was threatened by the Turks after the seizure of Constantinople, he found it increasingly difficult to protect Samos from the ravages of pirates. His solution was to invite the Samiotes to settle on Chios, and many did ... leading to a wholesale depopulation of the island. Samos remained almost deserted for nearly a century. Eventually, around the middle of the 16th century, the island found a new protector in the form of Kilitz Pasba, a Turkish admiral, who was keen to repopulate the island. He brought settlers from the island of Mytilini, from Pyrgos in the Peloponnese, and from Vourla in Asia Minor; these immigrants founded the villages of Mytilini, Pyrgos and Vourliotes. Other 'newcomers', from Kymi on Evia, settled at Koumeika.

the T-junction turn left, away from the coast. This road soon makes a curve to the right, so that you are travelling parallel with the coast road in a westerly direction. The road to Leka is the second narrow road off left, just before a modern hotel (also on the left). You now find yourself curling upwards on to a ridge, which leads to **Leka** (36.3km), close to Walks 17 and 20. If you would like to take a break at Leka, you might use the notes for Circular walk 6 on page 26.

Suggested detour: An interesting diversion between Leka and Kastania (the next village en route) starts on the road off to the right, about 2km beyond Leka. This will take you up to the villages of Nikoloudes and Kosmadeo, and will add 12km to your cumulative kilometres. On some old maps the two villages are shown in reverse order, but you can be sure that the first one reached is Nikoloudes (🖼). This village is situated in a wooded area and boasts the oldest and largest plane tree on the island, next to which is the village wash-house. This really is a lovely, picturesque backwater. Kosmadeo (♣✕🖼; Walks 19 and 21), at a higher altitude still, stands clear of the trees, perched high on a mountain, looking out to Kerkis. Return the way you came, appreciating the wonderful views (🖼) on your descent. Turn right on rejoining the main route.

The main tour continues straight on. Soon you will see **Kastania** (40.6km 🖼) tucked into the hillside ahead. Park just as you enter the village, in the square on the right (dominated by a very impressive wash-house). The square also provides a good view back down the valley in the direction of Karlovassi.

Leave Kastania as if heading back towards Leka, but turn right almost at once on a road opposite a chapel; it is signposted for Marathokambos. There are good views () as you drive along the side of the valley, across to Platanos and the foothills of the Ambelos range of mountains. After 4km turn right to **Marathokambos** (46.9km ♁▲▲♠✕), where Walk 21 ends. Once in the town, drive through until you reach a square, where the road left leads into the town centre. Park here if you wish to explore. To continue on to Ormos Marathokambos, keep straight ahead here.

Ormos Marathokambos (51.8km ▲▲♠✕), where Walk 15 ends, is reached after winding downhill for 5km. Stay ahead at the crossroads, where the new bypass goes right, and shortly turn left into the village — or keep on the main road which runs along the shore, with magnificent views to the stark inland mountains (). **Votsalakia** (**Kambos**; 55.8km ▲▲♠✕) is the starting point for demanding, but rewarding, Walk 16, which climbs Kerkis via the monastery of Evangelistria — the white building you can see on the side of the mountain amongst the trees (photograph page 103). Although the beach at Votsalakia (Kambos) is pleasant, we suggest you save your swim and picnic for either of the two quiet sandy beaches you will reach after just a few more kilometres.

It is well worth diverting to the lovely beaches of **Psili Ammos** (60.8km) or **Ormos Limnionas** (0.9km down the track off left, after 62.1km). Observe the disparity in the scenery between the north and south of the island, which is at its most apparent here. Enjoy the

Samos town

breathtaking views (📷) and the sense of omnipotence of the giant Kerkis range towering upwards in splendid but forbidding solitude. At **Kallithea** the road branches: the upper fork goes into the village itself and the lower one, still unsurfaced, to **Drakei** (79.8km ✕). Park at the entrance to the village, and wander round this interesting remote outpost. A diversion down the track to the left, on entering the village, leads to the fishing hamlet of Ag. Isidoros. Walk 18 ends at Drakei.

Although you have no choice but to return by the same route, you see the landscape from a different perspective as you drive along the side of the mountain with the seashore below. Continue back towards Marathokambos, skirting Ormos Marathokambos on the bypass. At the crossroads, where left leads up to Marathokambos, keep ahead. You are now heading in the direction of Koumeika, across the plain below Marathokambos, towards more gently-rolling hills. The track/road ascends through olive groves, *phrygana* and *macchie,* more or less following the coast. Reaching a road (114.4km), turn right down to **Balos** (116km ▲✕📷), an attractive spot for a swim and a picnic, with a surprisingly-long beach fringed with tamarisk trees. Short walk 15 ends here.

To reach Koumeika, return up the road out of Balos and past the track/road you came along from Ormos Marathokambos. The gently-smoking structures you may see on this road, looking like Iron Age dwellings, are charcoal-burners (see page 102). On reaching a road junction (118.3km), turn right to **Koumeika** (118.6km ✕) and continue through to **Skoureika** (123.9km). Both of these villages provide a restful haven where you can enjoy an ouzo in peaceful surroundings. From Skoureika return towards Koumeika for 2.2km until, just after crossing a small bridge, you can turn right up a steep narrow road to Neochori. As you climb there are good views (📷) to be enjoyed back towards the coast. The road skirts the edge of **Neochori** and continues its climb up to the main road, where you turn right (129.9km). In no time at all you are in **Pyrgos** (135.6km ▲▲✕📷⛩), from where you can pick up the notes for Car tour 1 on page 20, to return to **Samos town** (167.5km).

● Walking

The only real way to enjoy the superb landscapes on Samos is, as the Greeks would say, '*me ta podia*', with the feet! And it's your feet we want to direct into the hills, through carpets of pink and purple anemones, down valleys to coves and inlets, and through all the varied landscapes that the island offers. All the groundwork has been done, so there is no need for you to waste any time. Straight from day one of those all-too-short holidays, you can be out in the countryside enjoying every moment.

Combining all the footpaths, trails and tracks into walks which have character, highlights and variety gave us a lot of pleasure. But there is scope for even further variation. Look at the walks and the maps, and see if you can come up with new combinations. A number of walks, for example, maybe joined end-to-end, taking you across large stretches of the island. A word of caution: never try to get from one walk to another across uncharted terrain! Only link up walks by following paths described in these notes or by using roads and tracks; don't try to cross rough country (which might be dangerous) or private land (where you may not have right of way). *Never* attempt to cross military areas. (And never attempt to take photographs in such areas, even if you are only pointing your camera at the ground to photograph flowers. At the very least, you may have your film confiscated, resulting in the loss of some treasured pictures.)

There are walks in this book for everyone.

If you are only a **beginner,** or just in the mood perhaps for gentle walking, then go for the walks graded 'easy'. Be sure to check all the short and alternative walks, too; some are easy versions of the long hikes. If you are looking for walks of two hours or less, then browse through the circular walks for motorists (see pages 18-32 and the dotted purple routes on the walking maps). Many of these can be reached by bus just as easily as by car. For very easy walks to take you almost instantly into beautiful countryside, you need look no further than the picnic suggestions on pages 9 to 15.

Experienced walkers should be able to tackle any walk in the book, taking into account, of course, the season and the weather conditions. *Don't* attempt strenuous walks in high summer; *do* protect yourself from the sun and carry ample water and fruit with you. *Always remember that storm damage or forest fires could make some of the walks described in this book unsafe.* Always err on the side of safety: if you haven't reached one of our landmarks after a reasonable time, you must go back to the last 'sure' point and start again.

There is probably only one challenge that **expert walkers** will be anxious to notch up: Vigla on Mt Kerkis. From sea level to 1440m/4725ft is a tough walk, and it is essential that the weather conditions are perfect. As an appetiser, you can flex your muscles in the Ambelos range where, at times, you can almost imagine that you are tackling the Dolomites!

Guides, waymarking, maps

There are no official **guides** on Samos, but none is needed for any of the walks in this book. If you wish to do any further explorations on the Kerkis range outside the scope of this book, then an experienced companion with local knowledge is essential.

Most of our walks are easily followed, and many are now **waymarked**. In fact, waymarking is now so profuse that it has become confusing, so *do follow our directions at all times* and ignore other route markings that you might chance upon. Refer to the maps in the book if you are unsure about your onward route. *Remember too: signposts can disappear!*

Source material for the **maps** in this book has slowly improved over the years, as better information has become more readily available. Ordnance Survey standard is still not an option, but a recently-published map for Samos comes closer than anything else on the market: Road Editions has published a Samos map (No 210) at a scale of 1:50,000. This can be purchased on the island or from your usual map supplier.

Note our use of terminology: a *track* is wide enough to be motorable; *trail* has been used to denote a narrower route, whether grassy, cobbled or concreted. A *footpath* is obviously very narrow.

What to take

If you are already on Samos when you find this book, and you haven't any special equipment such as a rucksack or walking boots, you can still do many of the walks or you can buy the basic equipment at one of the sports shops in Samos town or Karlovassi. Boots can be bought quite cheaply from one of the shoe shops. Don't attempt any of the difficult walks without the proper gear or with brand-new footwear. For each walk in the book the *minimum* year-round equipment is listed. Where walking boots are required there is, unfortunately, no substitute: you will need to rely on the grip and ankle support they provide, especially on walks where the path descends steeply over loose stones. All other walks should be done with stout shoes, preferably with thick rubber soles, to grip on wet and slippery surfaces.

You may find the following checklist useful:

walking boots (which must be broken-in and comfortable
up-to-date bus timetable (from the bus station)
waterproof rain gear (outside summer months)
water bottle with water purifying tablets
long-sleeved shirt (sun protection)
long trousers, tight at the ankles (sun and tick protection)
rehydration packs (Dioralyte), especially if walking in hot weather
spare boot laces

compass, whistle, torch
first-aid kit, including bandages and band-aids
plastic plates, cups etc.
protective sun cream
anorak (zip opening)
knives and openers
sunhat, sunglasses
2 cardigans
antiseptic cream
insect repellent
small rucksack
woollen hat and gloves (winter)
extra pair of (long) socks
plastic groundsheet

Please bear in mind that we have not done *every* walk in the book under *all* conditions. We might not realise just how hot or exposed some walks might be in high summer or how cold in winter. For this reason we have listed under 'Equipment' all the gear you *might* need, depending on the season. We rely on your good judgement to modify the list accordingly.

Beware of the sun and the effects of dehydration. Don't be deceived by light cloud cover; you can still get sunburnt. It's tempting to wear shorts for walking — forgetting that, with the sun behind you, the backs of your legs (as well as your neck) are getting badly burned. Pushing through the prickly holly oak isn't fun in shorts either, so always carry long trousers and a long-sleeved shirt. Put them on when you have had enough sun, and *always* wear a sunhat. Take your lunch in a shady spot on hot days and carry a good supply of fruit and water.

Where to stay

We use Samos town as our walking base; it is a pleasant and popular place to stay, and all the buses run from there. If you choose to stay at one of the other major resorts on the island, like Kokkari or Pythagorion, or even Karlovassi, you will still be able to do the majority of the walks in this book using the public transport system. Two smaller south coast resorts, Ireon and Votsalakia, are fairly isolated; walking from these bases would be very limited. A hire car can solve the problems of getting around to see the island, but it restricts you to circular walks. Using taxis to link up with the main bus routes offers a practical and less costly means of enjoying a wider selection of walks from these isolated bases.

Outside peak season finding accommodation is not difficult and can add that extra dimension of freedom and cut down on some of the daily travelling. Contact Samos Tours, tel: 0030 273 27738; fax: 0030 273 28915.

Weather

The best months for walking on Samos are April to June and September to October. The summer months (mid-June, July, and August) are hot to very hot, with temperatures sometimes reaching 40°C/104°F. The only walking you are likely to want to do is back and forth to the beach or the bar!

Spring announces itself as early as February, with an increasing number of wild flower species around including orchids like *Barlia robertiana,* the giant orchid; but the weather is still very variable and unpredictable. March sees an even greater number of flowers carpeting the meadows, and the pink and mauve *Anemone coronaria* seems to be everywhere, but the weather is improving only slowly. April is the month to air the shorts and, given no worse than the average weather, you can expect to be out and about for most of the time enjoying a good deal of sunshine and the very best of the flowers — but there is still a chance of unsettled weather.

In May the weather settles towards its summer pattern, and the temperatures rise steadily. As the month progresses, the heat and lack of moisture persuades many of the lowland plants into their survival strategy, and it is now necessary to climb to higher altitudes to see the best of the flora.

The month of June sees the weather moving smoothly towards its summer heat and the prospects of rain limited to rare thunderstorms. The long hot summer persists well into September, when a short unsettled spell heralds a change. Temperatures now fall back to the 20s°C/70s°F, and the air feels fresh again.

October, like November, remains fresh and pleasant, with plenty of sunshine and a temperature high enough to wear shorts. Still, rainy periods are now increasingly likely. It is the rain which brings on the flush of autumn flowers like the cyclamen, the crocus and the beautiful yellow *Sternbergia lutea*.

Things that bite or sting

Dogs generally do no more than bark their warning, but when confronted by aggressive dogs, we find the 'Dog Dazer' invaluable. A Dog Dazer is an easily-portable electronic device which emits a noise inaudible to the human ear, but startles aggressive dogs and persuades them to back off. If you are interested in purchasing a Dog Dazer, contact Sunflower Books, who sell them. Otherwise, the best advice, if you feel threatened and you have no walking stick, is to pick up a stone and pretend to throw it.

Snakes are something you *will* have to watch out for but, fortunately, most of them are harmless except for the viper species, recognised by the diamond or blotched pattern along the back of the snake. The best advice is to move out of their way; they tend not to move out of yours. The real danger comes if you accidentally step on one and, for that reason, it is *imperative* that you do not walk in the countryside in open sandals, no matter how comfortable they are for walking! Always have your feet and ankles well covered. It is also a sensible precaution to wear your long trousers tucked into your socks. Most snakes are more frightened of you than you are of them and will move rapidly out of reach. Take special care near water, when you are about to sit down, or when you choose to rest your hand, so innocently, on a drystone wall. Snakes are most active throughout April and May and again, to a lesser extent, in October.

Scorpions are about too, but you are most likely to see them at the height of summer when they are usually seeking the shade, so don't leave any of your clothing on the ground. Accidentally turning over rocks and

! *Note that military activity is spasmodic, but remember that it may* affect *some* walks *very occasionally* — perhaps once a year.

stones may expose them, but generally they offer no serious threat: their sting is painful than danger-ous for most people.

Bees and **wasps** are around in summer so, if you are allergic to insect bites, make sure you always carry with you the necessary pills and creams.

Greek for walkers

In the majority of tourist areas you hardly need to know any Greek at all, but once you are out in the countryside a few words of the language will be helpful. Anyway, it is nice to be able to communicate, if only a little, and people warm to your attempts.

Here's one way to ask directions in Greek and understand the answers you get! First memorise the few 'key' and 'secondary' questions below. *Then, always follow up your key question with a second question demanding a yes (ne) or no (ochi) answer.* Greeks invariably raise their heads to say no, which looks to us like the beginning of a 'yes'! (By the way 'ochi' is usually given the hard pronunciation on Samos, ock-ee, and less often the softer o-hee, o-shee or oi-ee.)

Following are the two most likely situations in which you may need to use some Greek. The dots (...) show where you will fill in the name of your destin-ation. The approximate pronunciation of place names is given in the Index, starting on page 133.

- *Asking the way*

  The key questions

English	Approximate Greek pronunciation
Good day, greetings	**Hair**-i-tay
Hello, hi (informal)	**Yas**-sas (plural); **Yia**-soo (singular)
Please	Sas pa-ra-ka-**loh**
Where is	pou ee-**nay**
the road that goes to...	o **thro**-mo stoh ...
the footpath that goes to	ee mono-**pati** stoh ...
the bus stop?	ee **stas**-sis?
Many thanks.	Eff-hah-ree-**stoh** po-**li**.

  Secondary question leading to a yes/no answer

English	Approximate Greek pronunciation
Is it here/there?	**Ee**-nay e-**tho**/eh-**kee**?
Is it straight ahead/behind?	**Ee**-nay kat-eff-**thia**/**pee**-so?
Is it to the right/left?	**Ee**-nay thex-**ya**/aris-teh-**rah**?
Is it above/below?	**Ee**-nay eh-**pano**/**kah**-to?

■ *Asking a taxi driver to take you somewhere and return for you, or asking a taxi driver to collect you*

English	Approximate Greek pronunciation
Please	**Sas** pa-ra-ka-**loh** —
would you take us to ...	tha **pah**-reh mas stoh ...
Come and pick us up	**El**-la na mas **pah**-reh-teh
from ... at ...	apo ... stees ...

Point out on your watch the time you wish to be collected.

As you may well need a taxi for some walks, why not ask your tour rep or hotel reception to find a driver who speaks English. We'd also recommend that you

Enjoy some beautiful pastoral scenery along the centuries-old trail connecting Koutsi with Neochori (Walk 15).

use an inexpensive phrase book which gives easily-understood pronunciation hints as well as a good selection of useful phrases.

It's unlikely that a map will mean anything to the people you may meet en route. Doubtless, they will ask you '**Pooh pah**-tay?' — at the same time turning a hand over in the air, questioningly. It means 'Where are you going?' and quite a good answer is 'stah voo-**na**', which means 'to the mountains'.

Walkers' checklist

The following points cannot be stressed too often:

- **At any time a walk may become unsafe due to storm damage, forest fires or bulldozing**. If the route is not as described in this book, and your way ahead is not secure, do not attempt to go on.
- **Walks for experts** may be unsuitable in winter, and all mountain walks may be hazardous then.
- **Never walk alone**. Four is the best walking group.
- **Do not over-estimate your energies**. Your speed will be determined by the slowest walker in the group.
- **Transport connections** at the end of a walk are vital.
- **Proper shoes or boots** are essential.
- **Mists** can appear suddenly on the higher elevations.
- **Warm clothing** is needed in the mountains; even in summer take some along, in case you are delayed.
- **First-aid kit, compass, whistle, torch** weigh little, but might save your life.
- **Extra rations** must be taken on long walks.
- **Always take a sunhat with you**, and in summer carry a cover-up for your arms and legs as well.
- A **stout stick** is a help on rough terrain and to discourage the rare unfriendly dog.
- **Do not panic in an emergency**.
- **Read and re-read** the important note on page 2, the Country code on page 44, and the specific guidelines on grade and equipment at the beginning of each walk you plan.
- **Carry at *least* one litre of water per person in hot weather**.

Organisation of the walks

The 21 main walks in this book are grouped in three general areas: the east, the centre/north, and the west. You might begin by considering the large fold-out touring map inside the back cover. Here you can see at a glance the overall terrain, the road network, and the exact orientation of the walking maps in the text. Quickly flipping through the book, you will find that there is at least one photograph for each walk.

Having selected one or two potential excursions from the map and the photographs, look over the planning information at the beginning of each walk: here you'll find *our* walking times, grade, equipment, and how to get there and back. If the grade and equipment specifications are beyond your scope, don't despair! There's almost always a short or alternative version of a walk and, in most cases, these are less demanding of agility and equipment. If it *still* looks too strenuous for you, turn to the car tours, where the circular walks for motorists describe walks generally of less than two hours' duration or the picnics (pages 9-15), where very short walks are suggested.

When you are on your walk, you will find that the text begins with an introduction to the overall landscape and with comments on special points of interest, before describing the route in detail. The large scale maps (all 1:50,000 and all with north at the top) have been overprinted to show current routes and key landmarks. Times are given for the overall walk and for reaching certain landmarks. Note that **we are fit walkers** and that our times average between 3km/h and 6km/h. Also note that the times given are *pure walking times* and include only brief pauses. The most reliable way to use this book is *not* to try to match our times minute-by-minute, but to note the *time difference* to the next point on the route. **A walk may well take you at least twice as long as the stated time.** Don't forget to take bus connections at the end of the walk into account. You'll soon see how your pace compares with ours and make adjustments for your stride.

These symbols are used on the walking maps:

▬▬▬	main road	☛	spring, well, etc	☩	church, chapel
▬▬	secondary road	*P*	picnic suggestion (see pages 9-15)	†	shrine
▬▬	unsealed road			∩	cave
▬	jeep track	🗺	best views	⊹	cemetery
🚌1	circular walk for motorists	🚍	bus stop	▥	stadium
⋯⋯⋯		🚗	car parking	🏕	picnic tables
-------	path, steps	■□	building.enclosure	⚑	monument
2→	main walk	⋔	ancient site	⊕	hospital
2→	alternative walk	■	castle or fort	M	museum
		⚒	quarry	🏭	factory

Country code for walkers and motorists

The experienced rambler is used to following a 'country code' on his walks, but the tourist out for a lark may unwittingly cause damage, harm animals, and even endanger his own life. A code for behaviour is important wherever people roam over the countryside and especially so on Samos, where the rugged terrain can lead to dangerous mistakes.

- **Only light fires** at picnic areas with fireplaces. Stub out cigarettes with care.
- **Do not frighten animals.** The goats and sheep you may encounter on your walks are not tame. By making loud noises or trying to touch or photograph them, you may cause them to run in fear and be hurt.
- **Walk quietly** through all hamlets and villages and take care not to provoke the dogs. Ignore their barking and keep your walking stick out of sight. Remember, it is only to be shown to a menacing dog.
- **Leave all gates as you find them**, whether they are at farms or on the hillsides. They are meant to keep goats or sheep in (or out of) an area. Here again, animals could be endangered by careless behaviour.
- **Protect all wild and cultivated plants.** Don't try to pick wild flowers or uproot saplings. They will die before you even get back to your hotel. Obviously fruit and other crops are someone's private property and should not be touched. *Never walk over cultivated land.*
- **Take all your litter away with you.**
- **Walkers — DO NOT TAKE RISKS!** This is the most important point of all. Do not attempt walks beyond your capacity, and do not wander off the paths described here if there is any sign of mist or if it is late in the day. **Do not walk alone**, and *always* tell a responsible person *exactly* where you are going and what time you plan to return. Remember, if you become lost or injure yourself, it may be a long time before you are found. On any but a very short walk close to villages, be sure to take a first-aid kit, compass, whistle, torch, extra water and warm clothing, as well as some high-energy food, like chocolate.

1 KAMBOS • VOURLIOTES • MONI VRONDA • KOKKARI

See map on reverse of touring map; see also photograph page 22

Distance: 10km/6.25mi; 3h

Grade: moderate-strenuous. The walk starts with a continuous ascent from sea level up to 460m/1500ft, on a mainly good trail. The downhill section is often over rocky or stony paths unsuitable for fast walking.

Equipment: sturdy shoes or walking boots, sunhat, sunglasses, suncream, long-sleeved shirt, long trousers, cardigan, raingear, picnic, water, bathing things

How to get there: 🚌 from Samos to 1km past the Vourliotes junction (Samos-Karlovassi bus, Timetables 1, 1A; journey time 30min). Ask for the Paleohori/Svalas Beach junction. Frequent buses in summer; in winter there are suitable buses only on weekdays.
To return: 🚌 from Kokkari to Samos (Karlovassi-Samos bus, Timetables 1, 1A; journey time 17min). There are often extra buses running from Tsamadou Beach; see footnote to Timetable 1, page 129.

Short walks: The first two alternatives eliminate much or all of the uphill section. Equipment as above.

1 Vourliotes — Moni Vronda — Kokkari: 7.5km/4.7mi; 2h15min; moderate. 🚌 from Samos to Vourliotes (Timetable 6; journey time 45min). Or 🚌 to Kokkari (Samos-Karlovassi bus, Timetables 1, 1A) and a taxi on to Vourliotes (12km). Start the walk at the road signposted to Moni Vronda, at the eastern edge of the village.

2 Moni Vronda — Kokkari: 5.5km/3.5mi; 1h45min; easy. 🚌 from Samos to Kokkari as in Short walk 1 above, then taxi all the way to Moni Vronda (14km). Start the walk at the 1h22min-point.

3 Kambos — Vourliotes — Kambos: 5km/3mi; 1h30min; moderate. 🚌 from the Paleohori/Svalas Beach junction (as main walk) and return (Samos-Karlovassi bus, Timetables 1, 1A; journey time 30min). Walk up to Vourliotes and return the same way.

If you don't mind exchanging a cheery greeting with the hill farmers, then follow this walk to Vourliotes, one of the timeless and unchanging villages which

Moni Vronda (Walks 1 and 7)

nestle in the folds of the densely-wooded lower slopes of Mount Ambelos, the 'Vine Mountain'. Take your fill of wandering the narrow, sometimes stepped, streets of this traffic-free village, before continuing on to one of the oldest monasteries on the island. Then prepare yourself for a change of mood as you descend from the monastery through wooded valleys and along craggy ravines, down the ancient route once used by the monks themselves.

The bus stops *on request* by the junction of the trail leading up to Vourliotes from Kambos. Alight here and **start the walk** by heading up the narrow concrete trail on the far side of the old road: it starts between high walls and is signposted to Paleohori). You begin a long, steady uphill section. There is a welcome chance for a breather when **Profitis Ilias** is reached (**6min**; Picnic 1). From here the views out over the plain of Kambos to the sea and inland towards the steeply-terraced hillsides dotted with tall graceful cypress trees are certain to make you linger. Be sure to examine the interesting old frescoes inside this little white church.

Six minutes after leaving the church continue on the concrete path to the left; it runs into an old cobbled trail nine minutes later. As you climb steadily upwards there is the opportunity for a close look at the vineyards which produce the grapes for the island's famous *'Samaina'* wine, immortalised in the words of Byron 'dash down yon cup of Samian wine'.

The three springs, known locally as '**Source Pnacas**'* (with a seasonal taverna, Taverna Pnaka, in an exquisite setting) are reached in **22min**. Beyond here the old trail has been interrupted by a track. Keep

*An alternative route from Source Pnacas (see purple lines on the map) makes an interesting diversion via the small church of Ag. Pandelimon; it is also a pleasant diversion on Short walk 3 and adds only 0.5km/0.3mi; 6min to the overall distance and time. From Source Pnacas, retrace your steps and, in under a minute, go left on a path along the top of a terrace wall below Source Pnacas. Three minutes later, rise up onto a crossing track. Turn left, then immediately right, up a concrete track. A short steep climb takes you past a stone farm building on the left. As the track swings sharply left (7min), go right on a field track. Fork right almost at once, on a path along the top of a terrace, to reach **Ag. Pandelimon** a few minutes later. To continue, go up the cobbled path/trail to the left, beyond the church. Pass behind a new building down to the left and rise onto a narrow farm track. Go left briefly, then fork left on a path. You rejoin the main trail 17 minutes later (at the 33min-point in the main walk); turn right to reach **Vourliotes** nine minutes later.

heading uphill on the track, but whenever you can, locate old cobbled sections of trail, where you can take short-cuts off the loops of the track. Finally you merge with the track, which becomes concrete as it rises to the edge of **Vourliotes** (**42min**). Stay ahead (keeping right),

but soon fork up left to reach the village square (photograph page 22) two minutes later. There is a choice of tavernas, but the mixed plate of *mezedes* at 'Blue Chairs' is worth sampling.

Leaving Vourliotes, head for the eastern side of the village. Turn right up a narrow street, alongside a joinery workshop, just beyond a small car park on the left. Keep climbing until you meet a bend in the Moni Vronda road (on your left). It is necessary to follow the road for a time now, but look for a section of the old trail which leads off to the right, 15 minutes up from the village square, and follow this to rejoin the road higher up.

Moni Vronda is reached 30 minutes after leaving Vourliotes, **1h14min** into the walk. Normally the army has a small presence here, but keeps a low profile, and there are no problems taking photographs. To visit Moni Vronda, first pass the path down to Kokkari (your onward path) on the left of the entrance road to the monastery. Ignore the 'No Entry' signs, which refer to vehicles.

Then continue the walk down the well-waymarked concrete path to Kokkari, and keep ahead on a woodland path as the concrete ends. The open pine forest (badly burnt in summer 2000), which provides limited shade as you start your descent, is also the home of a rather unusual leafless orchid, *Limodorum aborvitum*. It is around for much of the spring and early summer, so watch out for its unmistakable tall purple spikes. In nine minutes you descend to a track: turn left to find the ongoing waymarked path, on the right, half a minute later. (Alternatively, keep ahead on the track and turn right six minutes later. In a further three minutes, as the track swings right, rejoin the main route by turning down left on a path.) Vistas open out as you reach a small clearing with a ruined farm building, 12 minutes after leaving the monastery. Follow the path past farm buildings, with the track down to your left, and descend

Kokkari

along terraces until the track is easily accessed. Turn left (or follow the track right in a U-bend round the valley, which takes an extra three minutes) and, in about one minute, take the path down right, to cross the valley (just before the track bends left). Take care rising up to join the track on the far side, and turn left to continue.

Minutes after rising from the stream bed, there is a dramatic change in scenery, as the track enters a ravine where vegetation gives way to a towering wall of barren rock. The track winds through the ravine, but soon there is a first sighting of Kokkari and the Samos peninsula beyond it. At around the **1h55min**-mark, as you emerge from the ravine, Walk 13 joins from the right. Less than a minute later, a large rocky platform on the left provides a good excuse for a rest and an opportunity to enjoy some superb views (but there is a slight danger of vertigo near the edge). Although Kokkari may seem very close, there is still a long way to go. You come upon another viewpoint three minutes further on; then the track becomes a stony path and heads down to meet a farm track (**2h11min**). (A left turn on this track descends to the 2h17min-point in the walk.)

The path continues opposite, descending steeply, to cross another track and a meadow, before rejoining the main track again (**2h17min**). Turn right, over a small concrete bridge, and follow this track down to a T-junction (**2h35min**). Turn right; then, almost immediately, go left on a path (at the right of a tree with a red waymarking dot), ignoring any chain which may bar your way. Follow the path downhill, to rejoin the track on a bend. Then keep heading downhill, to emerge on the edge of Kokkari at the BYPASS. Catch a bus here or walk a further 10 minutes along the shore road, into **Kokkari** (**3h**).

2 KOKKARI • VOURLIOTES • MANOLATES • STAVRINIDES • AG. KONSTANTINOS

See map on reverse of touring map; see also photographs pages 4, 22 and opposite

Distance: 16km/10mi; 4h

Grade: moderate-strenuous. The uphill sections of this walk total a surprising 600m/2000ft, but they are spread throughout the walk.

Equipment: sturdy shoes or walking boots, sunhat, sunglasses, suncream, long-sleeved shirt, long trousers, cardigan, raingear, picnic, water

How to get there: 🚌 from Samos to Kokkari (Samos-Karlovassi bus, Timetables 1, 1A; journey time 17min). Frequent buses in summer; in winter there are suitable buses only on weekdays.
To return: 🚌 from Ag. Konstantinos to Samos (Karlovassi-Samos bus, Timetables 1, 1A; journey time 37min).

Short walks

1 Kokkari — Vourliotes — Kambos: 7.5km/4.8mi; 2h; easy-moderate. Follow the main walk to Vourliotes and then use the map to descend to Kambos on the coast road via Source Pnacas and Profitis Ilias.

2 Kokkari — Vourliotes — Platanakia: 10km/6.3mi; 2h25min; moderate. Follow the main walk to Vourliotes and then walk on to Platanakia by picking up Walk 7 from the 2h30min-point (page 74). See also photograph page 25.

3 Kokkari — Vourliotes — Manolates — Platanakia: 14km/8.75mi; 3h10min; moderate-strenuous. Follow the main walk to Manolates and then walk on to Platanakia by picking up Walk 12 at the 3h09min-point (page 89). See also photographs pages 25 and 87.

The northern slopes of the Ambelos range are deeply folded and rich in vegetation. Rivers and streams rush, tumble and gurgle down valleys where oleander and plane trees jostle for a place by the water. In the deepest valleys ivy climbs silently to the very top of the highest tree and, just to provide that touch of romance, the air is filled by the sweet song of the nightingale. Our walk follows narrow, intimate and sometimes sunken footpaths, as they wind up and down the folds, in and out of the valleys, crossing rivers and streams along the way. Three sleepy hill villages are visited en route, each one a little higher than the last, before the time comes to return to sea level once again. We can do no better than echo the words of Theokritos to entice you:

> A vine spreads out its tendrils there, and bears
> its fruit in spring, the clear-voiced blackbird sings
> its lively tune and lilting nightingales return
> the song in honeyed notes. Go there...

The walk starts as you leave the bus in the centre

of **Kokkari**. Head west along the road, following the depart ing bus until, in **10min,** you reach the edge of the town. Cross the main road and head up the narrow surfaced road opposite, at the end of the bypass. When you reach a THREE-WAY JUNCTION (**13min**), fork right. (The concrete track to the left is followed in CW2 and is where Walk 1 ends; ignore the middle track.) Almost immediately, turn left above the greenhouses of an orchid nursery. The track passes under a rather curious bridge built onto a rock and leads immediately down to the first stream, just **16min** into the walk. Turn right along the stream bed, then head round left alongside a second, wider stream, which you can cross on stones. Follow the path half left, up the slope and away from the stream. Don't miss the point where the path heads up right (**24min**); it takes you to a track in under a minute. Now follow the waymarked path on the embankment diagonally left across the track (indicated by a cairn).

For a time this waymarked path continues over relatively soft bedrock which has been worn by the passage of many feet over many years into a smooth hollow. Look, too, for the footsteps cut into the rock, to help when there is a change of level. Follow the path alongside the valley, in a gradual ascent through denuded pine forest and *phrygana*. When you meet a track (**44min**), cross it and continue through a valley, recrossing the track at **49min**. (Alternatively, turn left at the 44min-point and follow the track in a semicircle to the right; when you reach the 49min-point, turn left on the path.) A clearing is reached in **55min**. The good views back over the wooded valley might tempt you into a picnic stop, but continue for two minutes to the beauty spot by the stream before you make your decision. Here sheer rock faces tower to the head and side of the valley; pines and cypress trees dot the landscape, and oleanders spread a pink profusion by the water's edge (Picnic 2a).

You might wonder, as we did on our first explor-ations, just how the route proceeds from here, but it is surprisingly easy and the climb is only 130m/430ft, so it is not as high as it looks. After crossing the stream the path becomes a trail and crosses a track (**1h10min**). When you reach a paved track, turn left and then right. On meeting a paved track again, continue left uphill. This track becomes a concrete road which leads to the main road left into **Vourliotes** (**1h20min**). Continue through the square (photograph page 22). *(But head downhill to descend via Source Pnacas and Profitis Ilias for Short walk 1.)* Take the third right turn, signposted to Manolates. Then, at the T-junction, go left; you reach the cemetery at the western edge of the village four minutes from the *platea*.

Pass to the right of the CEMETERY, to come upon a trail. It takes you down to an open area, where your waymarked path continues to the left (**1h26min**). Ignore a waymarked path down to the right over two minutes later, then reach a critical division of paths 12 minutes from Vourliotes (**1h32min**). Both paths here are waymarked, but ours is the one that heads sharp left. *(Keep right here for Short walk 2.)*

Cross a track to a small white CHURCH, reached **1h33min** into the walk, from which you can enjoy a clear view of our next destination, Manolates. Be sure to stay with the waymarked path, which continues round and beneath the front of the church. Leafy shade, filtered sun and lush green vegetation set the scene now, as you descend into this beautiful valley. Listen for the song of the nightingale. When you reach the RIVER in **1h45min**, head upstream for around 10m/yds, before you cross to pick up waymarks again on the opposite side. There is an ascent ahead of some

A Persian bead tree shades this fine old Byzantine church at Ag. Konstantinos. May 21st is the special day for St Constantine and is celebrated by all Greeks who bear his name. Saints' days take the place of birthdays in Greece, which means that most celebrations are on Maria's day, August 15th. Traditional gifts are cakes and flowers so, if you see ribbon-tied cake boxes and bouquets of flowers, you can be sure it's a saint's day!

200m/650ft, but at least you can enjoy the cool air in these sunken paths, which are so deep that they offer shade at all times. The mossy banks of these paths provide a good habitat for the dense-flowered orchid, *Neotinea maculata,* which has a flower so tiny that you'll need a magnifying lens to appreciate its miniature beauty.

All the cool and shade is left behind when the path runs into a grassy track (**2h03min**). Soon turn left at a T-junction of tracks, and continue uphill through the vineyards. Ignore the next left turn, but turn left at the junction nine minutes later. As you turn here, look for the continuation of the waymarked path on your right, reached in under a minute. The path soon reverts to track, but forks left uphill less than two minutes later. Soon you rejoin the track: go left and then right, to rise up onto the concrete track which leads up into **Manolates**. You reach the fountain in the centre at **2h21min**. The *kafeneions* in Manolates offer perhaps the last chance of refreshment before the end of the walk. (Stavrinides is particularly sleepy, although it does have a taverna.)

Head downhill from the fountain, then take the first left, a track. *(But continue ahead on the road here for Short walk 3.)* Keep along this track (photograph page 4) until you reach a fork in 10 minutes. Go right and follow the track round the contours, with the valley down on your right. On coming to a T-junction, turn right and, almost immediately, find the path to Stavrinides on the left (**3h09min**). Signs of cultivation indicate that Stavrinides is not too far away, but first you must cross a stream bed. Keep left to reach the centre of **Stavrinides** in **3h20min**. If you cannot find anywhere open, at least you can refresh yourself from the water tap by the church.

Retrace your steps past the church and turn left at the junction, to leave the village by the CEMETERY. The road reduces to a track from here. Pick up the waymarked trail on the left, about six minutes down the track. In three minutes, you meet the track again: turn left but, four minutes later, pick up the path again, on the right (keeping right initially). Five minutes later meet the track again: go left: your steep path leads down to the right in less than a minute. Four minutes later rejoin the track: again turn left; in under one minute the good path down right leads to **Ano**

Ag. Konstantinos (**3h54min**). Keep right into the village square, then turn left to join the road (photograph page 51) leading down to the coast road on the edge of the village (**4h**). There are picnic tables by the bus stop here (Picnic 2b), where you can await the bus back to base. Or turn right, then left, down to the shore, where there is a taxi and cafes/tavernas along to the right.

Crossing the rushing river below Manolates, at 1h45min into the walk

3 SAMOS • PROFITIS ILIAS • SAMOS

Distance: 5.5km/3.4mi; 1h55min

Grade: moderate. Initially the walk ascends from sea level to 400m/1300ft and, while the paths and tracks are generally good, loose stones underfoot can make parts of the descent tricky.

Equipment: sturdy shoes or walking boots, sunhat, sunglasses, suncream, long-sleeved shirt, long trousers, cardigan, raingear, picnic, water

How to get there and return: No buses are required for this circular walk which starts and ends in Samos town.

Alternative walks: These three alternatives provide an opportunity to visit the fishing hamlet of Ag. Paraskevi. Although the *macchie* constantly threatens to invade the path used in Alternatives 1 and 2, it is still used and waymarked. Alternative 3 is mostly along a good track, with modest climbs.

1 Samos — Profitis Ilias — Ag. Paraskevi: 6km/3.8mi; 1h48min; moderate. Pre-arrange for a taxi to collect you from Ag. Paraskevi. Follow the main walk to the 1h11min point. Keep ahead on the track here, ignoring the track right to Kamara. In 3min turn right on a well waymarked crossing path, heading towards the sea. It leads down through *macchie,* which may encroach in places, towards Ag. Paraskevi. Reach the track below in 1h35min and turn left. On meeting the road under a minute later, turn right to Ag. Paraskevi (1h48min).

2 Ag. Paraskevi — Samos: 5.1km/3.2mi; 1h17min; moderate. Take a taxi to Ag. Paraskevi. Follow the Samos road for 12 minutes, then turn left on the track signposted to Vlamari. A minute later, turn right up a well-waymarked path (invaded, nevertheless, by *macchie*). About 20min uphill, cross straight over a track and continue on the waymarked path, picking up the main walk at the 1h16min-point.

3 Kamara — Ag. Paraskevi — Samos: 13.6km/8.5mi; 2h45min; easy-moderate. Take a taxi from Samos town to Kamara (5km), and alight at the junction with the Ag. Zoni road. (If you want to shorten the walk by 7.5km/4.7mi; 1h25min, arrange for the same driver to collect you again at Ag. Para-skevi.) Continue ahead (east) from the Ag. Zoni road junction and, almost immediately head left uphill on a narrow concrete road, shortly reaching a large plane tree which marks the centre of the old village of Kamara. Take the waymarked track at the right of the tree. Four minutes later turn right on another track (the track ahead is Walk 4 back to Samos town). Skirting to the right of a small cultivated valley, ignore tracks left and right. Keep left (30min) where a track

View across Samos Bay to the Ambelos range after unseasonal snowfall (Picnics 3a and 3b). Lazarus (Walk 13) stands out as the distinct peak against the skyline in the centre of the photograph, while Profitis Ilias (Walk 12) is the broad, flattened summit to the left of Lazarus.

heads sharply back to the right. From here the track contours round the wooded hillside about 100m/300ft above the sea — a very scenic section. Keep an eye open for the small chapel of Ag. Haralambos down right (44min); it's an excellent picnic spot. Ignore a turn-off down to Galazio Beach (58min) and reach the church of Ag. Rafael (1h04min; cover photograph), where another path leads to an isolated section of Galazio Beach. Continue ahead and, as you wind uphill on a concrete road, you reach a pink house with black railings on the right opposite a high concrete wall (about 5min after leaving the church). Just past the house turn right downhill on a track. Ignore a track off right in under 4min. Your track bends left and right; as it bends left a second time, take the path descending ahead, to reach Ag. Paraskevi in eight minutes. From here follow the road out of Ag. Paraskevi, heading gradually uphill. Take the track on the left signposted to Vlamari and Profitis Ilias (1h47min). Keep climbing until you can turn right on a track (2h03min) which takes you down to the route of the main walk just three minutes later. From here, pick up the notes for the main walk from just after the 1h16min-point , to return to Samos town.

A lmost every church in Greece which is perched on a hill overlooking the sea is called Profitis Ilias after the prophet Elijah. This particular one, which enjoys a dominant position over Samos town, offers commanding views over the whole peninsula. Beyond the church, on the northern shore, lies the small hamlet of Ag. Paraskevi. The walk penetrates one of the few areas of the island where the natural vegetation is truly

typical of the eastern Mediterranean. Now that you have a chance to see them, watch out for two types of strawberry tree, particularly the eastern strawberry tree with its smooth red bark, and also for the shrubby wild olive which has played such a vital role throughout the development of civilisation in the region.

The walk begins at the STADIUM in **Samos town** (16 on the town plan on page 8: to get there, walk from the port past the Customs House, turn right, then take the second left into 28 Octovriou). Continue past the stadium for one minute, then keep ahead up a narrower road, where the main road turns sharp left. In a further minute, turn left up a steep concrete road just before some apartments. Keep uphill, then go right on the track rising behind the apartments. You pass a

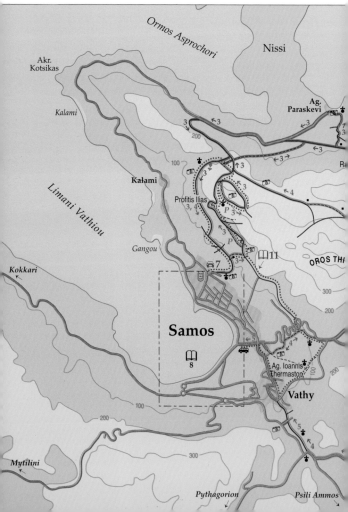

small church on the right, from where there are good views over Samos town. After passing a single-storey white building on the right, turn right onto a path marked with red paint dots (**11min**).

The waymarked path heads towards some iron fencing posts, but leads up to the right just before they are reached. As you climb steadily up this section, keep an eye open for the wild olive, which is just a smaller version of its cultivated cousin. Look around too, for already there are fine views over Samos town and Vathy, but these get better still as you climb. At around **19min**, when you emerge on a track, turn left. A couple of minutes later, just before a white SHRINE on the left, turn left back onto a footpath (but the less agile should keep ahead along the track). Follow the path

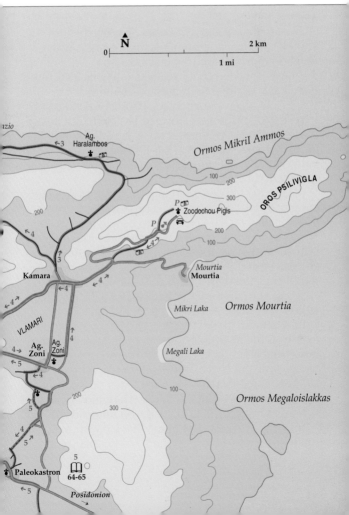

(Picnic 3a lies at the stone shelter by the edge of the pine wood here) until, as you approach the track again, the way is blocked by a fence. Go right on a faint path, 40m/yds *before* the fence, and curl left, then right, to clamber back onto the track (**34min**).

Turn left and continue up the track. Ignore the track joining from the right and the waymarked path also on the right immediately afterwards. At **44min** ignore a track forking down to the left (but note that it will be your ongoing route back to Samos town, after your visit to Profitis Ilias). Just past this track, look for a couple of red-marked trees on the right. Turn right here and climb straight up to a tall cairn. Once at the cairn, **Profitis Ilias** comes into view and is quickly reached (**55min**; Picnic 3b). From here the views are magnificent, with the coastline and offshore islands weaving a magic pattern.

To descend, follow the track starting behind the church, past some communication masts. At the T-junction of tracks four minutes later, turn left. Follow the track round the contours of the hill beneath Profitis Ilias, back to the 44min-point (**1h06min**). Here turn sharp right down the track. Ag. Paraskevi soon comes into view on the coast below. At **1h11min**, just before reaching the point where a track joins from the right (from Kamara; Walk 4), take the clear, waymarked path off to the left. *(But keep ahead on the track here for Alternative walk 1.)*

Follow the red dots and cairns as the path descends over stony ground in the direction of a solitary cypress tree ahead (which will turn out to be two trees in line). A minor waymarked path off left in under four minutes cuts a corner off the main path. The path joining sharply from the right a minute later comes from Ag. Paraskevi (*Alternative walk 2;* **1h16min**). Turn left on meeting a crossing track before reaching the cypresses (*Alternative walk 3 comes in from the right here*).

In **1h20min** pass a water storage point, known locally as the '**Hermit's Cave**', soon followed by steps down right to a small chapel. There are some fine views over the bay as the track descends gradually towards Samos town. The track leads down right to meet another track at a flat area (**1h40min**). Turn left towards Samos town, to reach the building first passed 11min into the walk (**1h45min**). Retrace your outward route from here down past the STADIUM (**1h55min**).

4 SAMOS • AG. ZONI • KAMARA • ZOODOCHOU PIGIS • KAMARA • SAMOS

See map pages 56-57; see also photographs pages 28, 54-55

Distance: 15km/9.3mi; 3h45min

Grade: easy-moderate. It is only the final pull up the hill to the monastery, Zoodochou Pigis, perched at an altitude of 300m/1000ft, which lifts this walk to just above the 'easy' grade.

Equipment: stout shoes or walking boots, sunhat, suncream, sunglasses, long-sleeved shirt, long trousers, cardigan, raingear, picnic, water

How to get there and return: No buses are required for this circular walk which starts and ends in Samos town.

Shorter walks: all are the same grade as the main walk, and all require the same equipment.

1 Samos — Zoodochou Pigis — Samos: 14km/8.75mi; 3h30min. Omit Moni Ag. Zoni and go directly to Zoodochou Pigis, by forking left instead of right at the 22min-point.

2 Samos — Zoodochou Pigis — Samos: 11km/6.8mi; 3h. Follow Shorter walk 1 above, but return to Samos the way you came.

3 Samos — Ag. Zoni — Samos: 10km/6.25mi; 2h35min. This walk leaves out Zoodochou Pigis and eliminates much of the climbing. Proceed via Ag. Zoni to the T-junction reached at the 53min-point), turn left on meeting the road, and then go right in 2min on a small concrete road. Now follow the main walk from the 2h11min-point.

Alternative walk: Samos — Ag. Zoni — Paleokastron — Samos: 8.5km/5.3mi; 1h45min; easy. This is a different route back to Samos from Ag. Zoni, via Paleokastron. From Moni Ag. Zoni return to the small cobbled road into Ag. Zoni hamlet (40min; first encountered just before the 38min-point). Head into the *platea* at Ag. Zoni, then go right up the concrete track. Turn left on a track (42min) and follow it in a curve below the white church (or take the steep path that skirts behind the church and climbs up to join the road at the 49min-point). When you meet the road (46min), turn right. Pass some dumped vehicles around 3min later (49min), where the road levels out. Follow the road, but fork right in 4min, onto a narrow road which reverts to track and passes a white house on the right (54min). Keep ahead on what is now a field track and soon reduces to path. The path crosses the middle of a field, drops down over shallow terraces, and reaches a gravel separation area (1h02min). Turn left here, and keep left at the fork. Ignore the track off left (1h05min) and reach the road 1min later. Turn right to Paleokastron square (1h08min). From here you can pick up the notes for Walk 5 (after the 2h19min-point, page 64) to get you back to Samos town. You can also include Zoodochou Pigis in this route: add 7.4km/4.6mi; 1h54min; moderate. From Ag. Zoni follow the main walk to Zoodochou Pigis, then return to Ag. Zoni to continue.

Skilful positioning of the island's monasteries gives them an enormous sense of tranquillity and solitude. It is almost as if a bargain has been struck with nature whereby these gifts, together with their commanding views, have been bestowed on the *monis* in return for their blending so unobtrusively into a landscape of great natural beauty. And so it is with Zoodochou Pigis. The views from there are regarded by some as the finest on the island. We reach it via an old trail. Only in the isolation of the final section, when there is the sound of goat bells around, do you feel a sense of history. Then you can almost imagine that you are leading a donkey train taking provisions up to the monastery. This walk also visits Ag. Zoni, another monastery, overlooking the cultivated plain of Vlamari. You need take only one step into the green interior to feel the solitude and tranquillity, and your voice falls to a whisper.

Start out from the BUS STATION in **Samos town** and, with your back to the sea, join the narrow concrete road ahead. Bear right as you leave this road; you reach a small square in **5min**. From here take the road left signposted for Vlamari, but watch out almost immediately for a concrete road forking off to the right: follow this to join an old trail a minute later. Campanulas in rich and pale shades of blue dot the way now, as you start to climb steadily up this old trail. In **11min** you meet the road on a bend, but continue up the old trail over to your right (by the side of a house). The views over Samos start to improve as you climb, but the best views are from the church near the top of the trail.

Continue ahead when the trail joins the road. On reaching a fork over three minutes later (**22min**), go right for Ag. Zoni. *(But for Shorter walk 1 bear left, to go directly to Zoodochou Pigis.)* The road takes you around two sides of the cultivated plain you now see on your left. While you are striding along the level, you might reflect on the question posted by Aristotle: 'Why are long walks on level ground more tiring than on uneven ground, but short ones less tiring?' Just before meeting a junction, you pass a narrow cobbled road off right (opposite a taverna) into **Ag. Zoni** HAMLET. *(The Alternative walk will return to this point.)* Turn left at the junction (**38min**), to come to **Ag. Zoni** MONASTERY on the right a minute later.

When you are ready to leave, turn right and right again, climbing the track by the side of the monastery (it is concreted at first). When you reach a T-junction (**41min**), turn left on a narrow concrete road which wends its way past farms, towards the village of Kamara. At the next T-junction (**53min**), turn right towards Zoodochou Pigis. *(But for Shorter walk 3, go left.)* Continue along the road which skirts the plain until a fork is reached seven minutes later. The route ahead leads down to Mourtia, but go left here, then take the clear cobbled trail off right a minute later. As you ascend

Car tour 3, Walk 4, Picnic 4: Zoodochou Pigis, one of the finest monasteries on Samos (see also photograph page 28).

quite steeply through the rocky terrain, keep an eye open for views down the eastern coastline of the island and across to the Turkish mainland. When the trail meets the road (**1h15min**), turn uphill. Four minutes later look for steps on the left which lead to a continuation of the old trail. Just two minutes up these steps you come to a shaded water source with seats. From here the climb becomes less steep, and the monastery is soon reached (**1h31min**). **Zoodochou Pigis** (Picnic 4; see above and page 28) is one of the finest monasteries on the island and is set in a commanding position. You can picnic on the outside terrace — seating is provided — and enjoy some really fine views.

From the monastery retrace your steps as far as **Kamara**. Keep ahead past the junction first encountered at the 53min-point. Two minutes later (**2h11min**) take the the small concrete road off to the right. (Or, if you are in need of refreshment, there are two tavernas a little further along the main road.) You reach Kamara *platea*, with its large plane tree, within a minute. From here take the waymarked track off to the right, towards a cultivated area. Ignore a track off to the right four minutes along *(the route of the Alternative walk 3-3)*; stay ahead, winding up towards a shallow saddle. Just before rising up onto the saddle, a path crosses your track diagonally (**2h39min**). Turn right on this waymarked path. Follow the waymarks carefully over the stony ground, passing a ruined stone shelter on the right. You descend to a rough track (**2h46min**) by another ruin: turn right here. Stay on the track now for some fairly level walking. You pass a clearing on the left and enjoy views down over Ag. Paraskevi below on the shore.

As you pass to the right of some old terraces below Profitis Ilias, you meet a T-junction of tracks (**3h01min**). Walk 20 paces left, to locate a strong path off to the right. Now pick up the notes for Walk 3 (from the 1h11min-point, page 58), to walk back to **Samos town** (**3h45min**).

5 MESOKAMBOS • MYKALI • PSILI AMMOS • PALEOKASTRON • SAMOS

Distance: 14.4km/9mi; 3h06min

Grade: easy. There is little climbing on this walk, which skirts the seashore and follows good tracks.

Equipment: stout walking shoes, sunhat, sunglasses, suncream, long-sleeved shirt, long trousers or shorts, raingear, picnic, water, bathing things

How to get there: 🚖 taxi or 🚌 from Samos to Mesokambos (Samos-Pythagorion bus; Timetables 4, 4A; journey time 12min). Alight at the track on the left, signposted to the small church of Pros Panagia Eleousa by the shore. (The driver maybe unsure of the stop, so be ready to alight 1.3km/0.8mi after crossing the river *(potami)* at Mesokambos, beyond a BP garage on the left and the Ouzo Samos distillery on the right, where the high white retaining wall on the right ends at the top of a long straight incline.)

Alternative starting point: Alight from the bus or taxi at the river in Mesokambos (see above). Start out by walking down the road signposted to Hotel Oceanida, with the river on your right. This is a good area for bird-watching in spring. In 10min keep right at a fork. Six minutes later do not swing right to cross the bridge: keep ahead on a track leading to the shore. You join the main walk at the 13min-point, where the river meets the sea. Turn left to continue. This option adds 0.6km/0.4mi; 6min.

Short walk: Psili Ammos — Paleokastron — Samos: 9km/5.6mi; 1h55min. 🚌 to Psili Ammos (Timetable 5; journey time 20min). Buses only operate in high summer; at other times take a taxi for this 9km journey. Pick up the main walk at the 1h11min-point.

Alternative walk: Mesokambos — Psili Ammos — Paleokastron — Ag. Zoni — Vathy: 14.4km/9mi; 3h25min. Follow the main walk to the 2h19min-point (just past the Byzantine-style church on the left). Turn right on the concrete track to Ag. Zoni. Use the map overleaf to walk to Ag. Zoni and then down to Samos town (Alternative walk 4 follows this route, in the opposite direction). This variation can also be added to the Short walk from Psili Ammos (9.5km/6mi; 2h15min).

If you love golden sandy beaches, then head for a 'Psili Ammos'; it means 'fine sand', and there is a good chance that you will find a pleasant beach. There is a fair chance, too, that you will have a number to choose from, for this descriptive name does tend to be over-used, but at least there are only three on Samos. This particular Psili Ammos is located on the south coast just to the east of Pythagorion and is almost within hailing distance of Asia Minor. It is one of the island's finest beaches, and located in a natural beauty spot (Picnic 5). The beach itself is still relatively unspoilt, especially earlier in the year, despite increasing development. It makes a pleasant spot for a swim or lunch in one of the tavernas.

This walk brings you back to Samos town through a different view of the Samos landscape. En route it is interesting to see some of the aspects of olive grove management. The fruit is harvested throughout the autumn and winter months, and whether the olives are beaten down or allowed to fall from the tree depends on the variety. Samos has a speciality olive which is not grown for its oil, but for eating; it is called *hamades*. These are allowed to fall from the tree into collecting nets, so it is important that the ground beneath the trees is clean. As you walk, look at the groves to check their upkeep and to see if the trees are well pruned. By the time you reach Paleokastron you may be ready to try a few olives with an ouzo perhaps? Well, why not, all you have to do now is roll down the old trail back into Samos.

Start out by walking down the track (initially concreted) signposted '**Pros Panagia Eleousa**'. As the track sweeps right on reaching the coast, take the path off left, towards the clutch of summer houses lining the shore at **Potami**. (Or first keep on the track to visit the chapel.) Just beyond the summer houses, the river *(potami)* from Mesokambos meets the sea (**13min**). At this point a diversion may be necessary in winter, to cross the bridge a few hundred yards inland. Ahead lies the wide sweep of the bay, with Psili Ammos out of sight behind a small hill.

The walk skirts behind the shore in the direction of Psili Ammos, either on path or rough track — rarely along the stony shore itself. Where a section of track ends at some greenhouses (**28min**), continue along the shore. Turkey lies close by across the water, Samsun Mountain within Dilek National Park providing a dramatic backdrop which becomes ever closer on the walk around the bay. In spring, flowers brighten the way

The flamingo lake at Psili Ammos

with swathes of colour, and you will often see a surprising number of migratory birds.

Keep ahead on meeting the bend of a road (**39min**) at the small resort of **Mykali**. In three minutes, as the road ends, again keep ahead, past summer tavernas and hotels. The road now runs parallel with the track, but stay along the shore until you have no option but to go left and join the road (**52min**). Turn right on the road to Psili Ammos, which edges the flamingo lake. A flock of wild flamingoes takes up residence on the lake in spring and stays as long as the water remains — usually until May. Whether you will see the flamingoes is very much dependent on winter rainfall. (You may not even spot the lake in summer, when it dries up and is used as a car park.) **Psili Ammos** is soon reached, as the road swings back towards the sea (**1h11min**).

For the next stage of the walk, to Paleokastron, start up the road from the beach. In less than one minute, take the trail to the right (signposted to Metamorphose). Climb some steps on the left two minutes later, to join a path. Pass a church on the left, then take the path which forks up left just before a white-walled water source. On rising up onto a track (**1h16min**), turn left. Now you can relax from route-finding for a time. Just continue ahead, ignoring all tracks joining from the left. The way goes above and around the back of the flamingo lake before turning inland. Before you lose sight of the south coast, there are some fine views to relish back down towards Psili Ammos and across to Turkey. Then the way becomes more pastoral, with olive trees and later cypresses weaving their own patterns into the landscape.

In **2h12min** meet the road and turn left for Paleokastron. The fork left in four minutes leads to the centre of Paleokastron and the tavernas, but keep ahead. In **2h19min** you pass a concrete track off to the right (just beyond a Byzantine-style church on the left). (*The Alternative walk heads right on this concrete track, which leads to Ag. Zoni.*) Two minutes past the track you reach the square at **Paleokastron**, with a water tap; a left turn here leads up into the village.

To make for Vathy and Samos, turn right to leave the square and follow the road for a time, keeping right at the Psili Ammos road junction

Kokkari

Mytilini

Mytilini

6
67

Pythagorio

(**2h33min**). Pick up the start of the old trail to Vathy on the right a minute later, just past a supermarket. It starts as a concrete road, but changes to a cobbled trail as it descends to Vathy. Five minutes down the trail, you cross a small road: it is worth diverting left to the main road here for a few moments, to enjoy a tremendous view down over Samos town. Continue down the trail until you enter **Vathy**, where you take the first street down left (with the wide central channel). Then bear right to enter a small square. From here turn left to head back into Samos. The square with the plane tree, where the road leads off to Vlamari, is reached in **2h56min**, and the main square on the seafront in **Samos town** ten minutes later (**3h06min**).

6 MYTILINI • AG. TRIADES • MONI SPILIANIS • PYTHAGORION

Distance: 13.8km/8.6mi; 2h50min

Grade: easy. The walk is on good tracks over level ground almost all the way. However, the descent on a dusty path can be tricky.

Equipment: sturdy shoes, long trousers or shorts, long-sleeved shirt, sunhat, sunglasses, suncream, raingear, picnic, water, bathing things

How to get there: 🚌 from Samos to Mytilini (Timetables 4, 4A). This service is a circular route via Samos, Pythagorion and Mytilini; it is also operated in the opposite direction: Samos, Mytilini, Pythagorion. Journey time Samos-Mytilini direct, 28min; via Pythagorion 40min (fares higher on this route). There are many daily departures in summer; in winter there are no Sunday departures.
To return: 🚌 from Pythagorion to Samos (Timetables 4, 4A; journey time 20min, or 43min via Mytilini). Ample daily departures in summer; in winter no Sunday departures.

Shorter walks: All three are easy, require the same equipment and use the same bus service (Timetables 4, 4A) as the main walk.

1 Ag. Triades — Moni Spilianis — Pythagorion: 8.5km/5.3mi; 1h45min. Take a taxi from Mytilini to Ag. Triades (4km) and begin there.

2 Mytilini — Ag. Triades — Mytilini: 9.7km/6mi; 2h. Follow the main walk to Ag. Triades and from there return by the road, to meet the main road on the southern side of Mytilini; turn right to head back into town.

3 Pythagorion — Moni Spilianis — Evpalinos Tunnel — Pythagorion: 5km/3.1mi; 1h. 🚌 to Pythagorion, rather than Mytilini. Follow the signposted road from Pythagorion to Moni Spilianis. To return, pick up the main walk at the 2h16min-point.

This gentle stroll is full of interest and, if you try it as an aperitif to your holiday, it will certainly whet your appetite for more. Alternatively, if you are looking for a relaxing day between mountain hikes, then this stroll is ideal. The walk heads first to the monastery of Ag. Triades. (Proper dress is required; see caption overleaf.) The old walls surrounding Pythagorion, built by Polykrates, provide the next focal point. You have fine views of them first, as you approach and, later, as you cross them to descend to another monastery, Moni Spilianis. Arriving at this second monastery, we were reminded of the quote from the Greek sage Palladas:

If solitaries, why so many?
so many, how are they then sole!
O crowd of solitaries feigning solitude.

Before you leave this monastery, be sure to visit the chapel inside the cave; it's a must. Last, but by no means least, visit the Evpalinos Tunnel, before continuing down to Pythagorion for a taverna lunch,

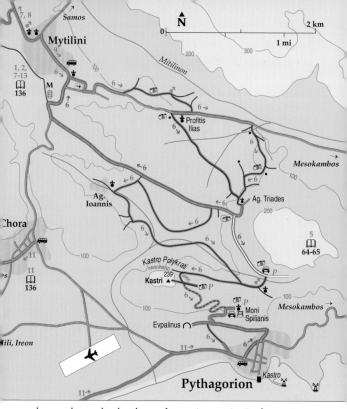

perhaps along the harbour front. It was in Pythagorion that we encountered evidence of a modern Greek philosopher: the opening hours on his shop door read 'Open mornings 10-12 and afternoons 2-4, or according to my whim'.

The bus stops by a shelter, opposite the small police station in **Mytilini**. **Start the walk** by heading southeast along the main street towards Pythagorion. Pass the old post office on the left (large yellow post box on the wall). One minute later, go left into a narrow concrete road, passing a blue church on the left, then a car park and CEMETERY on your right. Follow the road round to the right and, where you meet another road at a bend, go left. Take the next left turn (**6min**) and head downhill on a wide tarmac road. In **12min** fork left on a track (initially concreted), by a white house on the left-hand corner. (A large sign here indicates the way to a timber supply depot.) Continue ahead to pass the timber depot on the left and, soon afterwards (**16min**), at a fork, go uphill to the right. This delightful narrow and stony track climbs past a wall of rock on the left. Sea views appear ahead as the way descends through olive groves and past small farms. At a junction of tracks by a water tank (**23min**), turn right to skirt round a narrow valley on the left. Ag. Triades comes into view ahead as the main track swings right (**31min**). You meet the road one minute later, opposite a white house.

Turn left along the road. (Or, for a pleasant viewpoint and picnic spot, turn right and, in just over a minute, opposite a row of cypress trees, go left up a path. The path leads to the small white church of Profitis Ilias, a diversion which adds six minutes to the overall time. See map for an optional route from there to Ag. Triades.) Just before a bridge, seven minutes along the road, turn right on a concrete track. Take the second fork to the right a minute later, then ignore further forks off right. The track rises through pine wood to a crest (**48min**). Ag. Triades is seen ahead as the track descends. Two minutes later, when the main track swings left, take a lesser track down to the right. Mytilini can be seen ahead as the track descends and passes to the right of a farm building with a corrugated iron roof. Continue left below this building, now on a faint field track, which bends right and left, then crosses a shallow gully on a level stone bridge. Still on a faint stony field track, rise up alongside the terrace wall of an olive grove to the left, soon meeting a

As you leave the church and monastery at Ag. Triades heading for Picnic 6a (an optional shorter route highlighted in purple on the map) look behind you for some superb views. If you want to look around inside the monastery, it is open from 8-12 in the morning and 4-6 in the afternoon. The nuns strictly enforce the dress requirements: no shorts or (for women) trousers, culottes, or immodest dress. For ladies the problem is easily solved by slipping a skirt over what you are wearing. One or two skirts are available at the door but, if these are in use, you will have to wait for someone to leave. Taking your own saves time.

crossing track (**56min**). Turn left towards Ag. Triades, and ignore a wide track joining from the left a few minutes later. The track skirts below the monastery. (The track used for the optional route shown on the map comes in from the right.) Rise up beside **Ag. Triades** (**1h05min**), and go left to the entrance.

When you are ready to leave, retrace your steps from the front door to the corner and continue ahead on the road, passing in front of the church. Follow the road round to the right. You pass a motorable track off left in two minutes — another optional, shorter route via Picnic 6a (see map). The pine wood is left behind as the road descends. Ignore a track off left, but take the next track left, less than a minute later (**1h11min**). Polycrates' walls can be seen on the hill ahead before the track descends to the right, onto a cultivated plain. At a major crossing track (**1h23min**) turn left and pass a white building. At a further crossing track (**1h27min**), turn left again. (An interesting diversion here is the tiny hamlet of Ag. Ioannis to the right.) Stay with this track as it crosses a stream bed on the right and rises into the pine wood. At another crossing, less than eight minutes later, turn left and continue along a wide woodland track, to the right of a valley. The track passes close below Polycrates' walls up to the right. At the next

junction (**1h55min**), continue to the right. (A diversion left at this point leads past an interesting white church, a good picnic spot, and in three minutes to Picnic 6a.)

From here the track gently ascends the hillside. You have a fine opportunity to examine the ancient walls before you actually pass through them. The sea comes into view ahead as you rise up onto a crest on the slopes of **Mount Kastri** in **2h06min**. Two red arrows painted on the rocky ground diagonally ahead at this point indicate the onward path. To reach the summit continue up the track to the right, but for a beautiful picnic spot with good views towards Asia Minor, head left (Picnic 6b).

Return to the 2h06min-point and locate the red arrows to descend. The waymarked path curves first to the left then descends in long zigzags, heading in the general direction of Pythagorion castle. This 100m/330ft descent on a rather stony and dusty path is the only tricky part of the walk. If you can spare a glance from where you are carefully placing your feet, the early summer visitor has a chance of seeing the pyramidal orchid, *Anacamptis pyramidalis,* which abounds on these hillsides. You join the road at the approach to **Moni Spilianis**. Turn left to visit the monastery (**2h16min**; Picnic 6c) and be sure to enter the cave to see the chapel.

Leave the monastery by the road, passing a modern amphitheatre on the ancient theatre site. On coming to a road junction, turn right to visit the **Evpalinus Tunnel** in a further five minutes. Or, to return directly to Pythagorion without visiting the ancient tunnel, go right then immediately left, down a rough track through the fields. The track later becomes concreted. Reach the main road and turn left back to the centre of **Pythagorion** and the bus stop (**2h50min**).

A day on the beach

If you enjoy relaxing on a beach as part of your holiday, you have a wide range of walks from which to choose. Walk 5 visits Psili Ammos, walk 6 ends at Pythagorion, from where you can continue west out of town to the beach, and Walk 11 enjoys a fair stretch of beach-walking, so it is easy to stop for a dip. There is a beach at Votsalakia (Walk 16) although you might not find time to swim if you walk up nearby Mt Kerkis! Walks 17, 18, 19 and 20 all pass through Potami; walk 18 visits two of the finest beaches on the island, Mikro and Megalo Seitani, and walk 20 reaches as far as Mikro Seitani.

7 MYTILINI • (KASTRO LOULOUDES) • MONI VRONDA • VOURLIOTES • PLATANAKIA

See map on reverse of touring map; see also photographs pages 15, 22, 25, 45

Distance: 16.2km/10mi; 3h40min (+ 30min for Kastro Louloudes)

Grade: moderate. The height gained throughout this walk totals around 460m/1500ft, but the ascents are not too steep; otherwise the walk is on tracks and paths which are good underfoot.

Equipment: walking boots, long trousers, long-sleeved shirt, sunhat, sunglasses, suncream, picnic, water; warm clothing, woollen hat and gloves outside high summer

How to get there: 🚌 from Samos to Mytilini (Timetables 4, 4A). This service is a circular route via Samos, Pythagorion and Mytilini; it is also operated in the opposite direction: Samos, Mytilini, Pythagorion. Journey time Samos-Mytilini direct, 28min; via Pythagorion 40min (fares higher on this route). There are many daily departures in summer; in winter there are no Sunday departures.
To return: 🚌 from Platanakia to Samos (Karlovassi-Samos bus, Timetables 1,1A; journey time 35min). Daily departures in summer; in winter no Sunday departures.

Alternative walks: There are several different ways to end this walk, and three examples are given below (grade and equipment as above for all three). Remember to add 30min to the overall time if Kastro Louloudes is included with any of these alternatives.

1 Mytilini — Moni Vronda — Kokkari: 16.1km/10mi; 3h30min. Follow the main walk to Moni Vronda (2h), then walk on to Kokkari, using the notes for Walk 1 from the 1h22min-point (page 47). The bus back to Samos departs from Kokkari 16min after departing Platanakia.

2 Mytilini — Moni Vronda — Vourliotes — Kambos: 14km/8.7mi; 3h12min. Follow the main walk to Vourliotes (2h30min) and from there use the map to descend to Kambos on the coast via Source Pnacas and Profitis Ilias. The bus back to Samos departs Kambos just 3min after departing Platanakia.

3 Mytilini — Moni Vronda — Vourliotes — Kokkari: 17.8km/11mi; 3h50min. Follow the main walk as far as Vourliotes and from there go on to Kokkari by reversing the start of Walk 2 (refer to map). The bus to Samos departs from Kokkari 16min later than Platanakia.

Marked on every map of Samos is an old castle, Kastro Louloudes, shown to be somewhere in the region southwest of Kokkari. Our eyes were alert as we walked through the area, but we found no trace of it. We explored the region many times and still found no signs of it, so our curiosity just grew and grew, until finding it became a dedicated quest. Questions brought vague answers, everybody seemed to know of it, but nobody had actually seen it; nobody, that is, until we asked Triandafilos. Triandafilos had been born and raised in the nearby village of Vourliotes, and as a boy he sometimes played in the ruins of the old castle. His romantic description left us more deter-

71

mined than ever to find it. The castle, he said, is perched on the pinnacle of a hill looking down over Kokkari, and the only possible approach is by steps hewn into the rock-face centuries ago when the castle was built. The steps, he warned, blend so perfectly into the landscape, that it is 'doubtful that you will ever find them, even if I tell you where to look'. We did find the steps, thanks to an unknown goatherd who led us to the very spot; even then, only after looking at the rock face for a time could we spot the steps. The castle at last, and what a marvellous location! But all this is just the icing on the cake, for this walk has much to offer besides in the way of fine mountain scenery. If you have walked on the north side of the Ambelos range, you will realise what a new and different perspective is given by this southeastern approach, where the undulating mountains, softly wrapped and cloaked in green, beckon irresistibly.

The walk starts as you leave the bus in the centre of **Mytilini**. Head northwest towards Samos town for two minutes and then take a left turn, signposted to Kokkari. Follow this road uphill past a church and then another church, Ag. Dimitrios (with a water tap). The road gradually curves to the right, heading out of the town. In **9min** continue straight ahead where a road joins from the left (Walk 9), and enjoy open views as you start into a gentle ascent. The road soon reverts to track, but in **19min** be ready to go off left on the second of two tracks which lie close together just before the main track starts to descend. (But go straight on here for Walk 8.)

Now, as you ramble on through the olive and pine, where the display of spring flowers hides orchids such as *Orchis anatolica,* the skyline is dominated by two major peaks, Profitis Ilias and Lazarus, which come into a particularly fine perspective just before you reach a stream (**37min**). Here a huge plane tree spreads its mighty branches; you might be tempted to picnic.

From here the ascent steepens a little, but not appreciably, until you come to a fork (**59min**). Bear right here (Walk 10 joins from the left). As your pace slackens now, at least you'll have more time for tortoise-spotting as you pass over this rocky terrain; it's an area where we found them several times, so you might be lucky. Just as the track crests the hill (**1h16min**), stay left (Walk 10 departs on the right), and

View down over Kokkari from the walls of Kastro Louloudes

prepare to enjoy views of the north coast the moment you are clear of the pine forests. Stay left one minute later, and spare a moment to look back here for some fine views of Cape Kotsikas on the peninsula near Samos town. Another good viewpoint is reached in **1h26min,** but this time you will have to scramble up the stones on the right to enjoy it. The track continues steadily through fairly open pine until, in **1h39min**, the closest approach to **Kastro Louloudes** is reached. The castle is located on the very top of the mountain peak now on your right, but nothing can be seen of it from this viewpoint.

Kastro Louloudes diversion (30min return): Stay with the track as it passes close to the side of the mountain, but leave it at the point where it swings away to the left. Climb the bank on the right and follow a goats' trail to work your way round the base of the summit until you have reached the seaward side. Pass through the gap in the rocky out crop (rather like a gap-stile), to continue along a path which rounds the peak until the way is barred by a jutting rock: now turn upwards to scramble the last few metres through the bushes, to reach the rock-face. Be sure to head for the small gully. The hewn steps which lead up to the castle are on the right of the gully and start only at eye level; it might take a minute for you to see them. It takes only a few moments to scramble up to the castle, but it is not a place for those who dislike heights, as there is a danger of vertigo. The castle's location is truly magnificent (see photograph above), but so exposed to the elements that you wonder how the inhabitants survived. Return the same way to the track.

As you continue along the track, the pine woods

disappear, to be replaced by beautifully-cultivated vineyard terraces; they impart a neat order to the countryside. Soon, in **1h40min**, the highest point of the walk is reached (550m/1800ft) and, almost immediately into the descent, Moni Vronda comes into view. Crossing the path of Walk 13 (**1h49min**), you reach **Moni Vronda** in **2h03min**. If you picnic here, you can take advantage of the tables outside the main door, overlooking the northern shore. There is water inside the monastery grounds. From here Vourliotes is reached by following the road as it winds downhill but watch out, six minutes after leaving the monastery, for the section of old trail on the left which eliminates some road-walking. The square in the heart of **Vourliotes**, reached in **2h30min**, is so peaceful that it is hard not to linger a while.

The final section of the walk leads along a way-marked path down to Platanakia and starts from alongside the cemetery on the western edge of Vourliotes: continue through the square, to leave in the opposite direction from your arrival. Take the third street downhill on the right and turn left at the T-junction. Pass the cemetery on your left and head down the concrete/cobbled trail, to reach an open area five minutes below the square. Go left onto a path, and ignore the way-marked path down to the right in under three minutes. In **2h42min** you reach a critical division of paths which is *easily missed*. Keep right here. (Walk 2 goes left here.) Ignore minor paths off left, but at **2h47min** take the left fork. Nine minutes later, watch carefully for a short section of low curving wall on the right, which *may* be waymarked. Turn sharp left here, to pass in front of a farm building and into the next valley.

Soon, in **3h25min,** the path leads down to the floor of the **Valley of the Nightingales** and into a beautiful meadow bounded by the tree-lined river on one side and wooded and rocky slopes on the other. It is a lovely setting (Picnic 7; photograph page 25). Crossing the river by the stepping stones, you emerge two minutes later on the surfaced road, where you turn right to head back to the coastal road and the bus stop at **Platanakia** (**3h40min,** or **4h10min** if you visited Kastro Louloudes).

8 MYTILINI TO KOKKARI

See map on reverse of touring map; see photograph page 48
Distance: 9km/5.6mi; 1h55min

Grade: easy. There is little climbing involved in this walk, which follows good tracks all the way.

Equipment: stout shoes, long trousers or shorts, long-sleeved shirt, sunhat, suncream, sunglasses, raingear, picnic, water, bathing things

How to get there: 🚌 from Samos to Mytilini (Timetables 4, 4A). This service is a circular route via Samos, Pythagorion and Mytilini; it is also operated in the opposite direction: Samos, Mytilini, Pythagorion. Journey time Samos-Mytilini direct, 28min; via Pythagorion 40min (fares higher on this route). There are many daily departures in summer; in winter there are no Sunday departures.
To return: 🚌 from Kokkari to Samos (Karlovassi-Samos bus, Timetables 1, 1A; journey time 17min). Daily departures in summer. In addition, there are often buses running from Tsamadou Beach back to Samos, see footnote to Timetable 1. In winter no Sunday departures.

Alternative walk: Mytilini circuit: 11.5km/7.1mi; 2h35min. Follow the main walk to the 35min-point, then take the track up left onto the ridge. Keep on the ridge track towards the Ambelos mountains (you pass the track followed in Walk 10, off to the right, around 35min along the ridge). Go through the cutting and descend to a junction of tracks (1h15min). Turn down left here to return to Mytilini (see map; you are following Walk 7 in reverse).

Enjoy a changing vista with every step as you wander through the quiet countryside bordering the eastern edge of the Ambelos mountains. The host of wild flowers includes, as always, a good selection of orchids. The ubiquitous yellow bee orchid, *Ophrys lutea,* is one that the spring visitor can expect to find. Wild asparagus (see recipe page 105), too, is not uncommon, but the most succulent grows near water.

Start out by following Walk 7 (page 72), but in **19min** keep on the main track, to continue ahead. The track becomes concreted for a while as it descends.* Ignoring the track straight ahead, swing right in the bottom of the valley, to pass a shrine on the left dedicated to St. Barbara, Protector of Artillery. Then rise up to a junction (**28min**). Turn left here to continue; a RESERVOIR is on your right. Keep ahead as the track rises away from the reservoir, to pass a signposted track off left to Vourliotes (**35min**). *(The Alternative walk goes left here.)* Ignore other side-tracks and a left fork (**47min**); stay with the track as it bends right and crosses a stream bed two minutes later. Views of the Ambelos

---

*You will pass a trail off right on this section: it cuts off a loop in the track. If you take it, turn left when you rise to a track, immediately coming to the 28min-point in the walk. Turn right to continue.

Mountains become obscured by pines as you head away from the olive groves.

The highest point of the walk (250m/825ft) is attained in **1h03min**, just before you reach a five-way junction of tracks where the mountains come into view again. (Walk 10 joins here from the left.) Keep ahead on the upper track (not the lower parallel track which dips down), to pass a ramshackle smallholding on the right. A different type of wild gladiolus is seen here, *Gladiolus illyricus,* which is smaller than the more usual field gladioli, but still brandishing the same sword-like leaves which give the genus its name. When the track sweeps right, cut off a loop by heading down a path through the pines, then continue across the track to cut off a further loop. Turn right on rejoining the track, to meet a diagonal crossing of tracks (**1h11min**). Go down the path off left here, into a wooded valley. Less than five minutes later, turn left and then right, to negotiate two path junctions. In less than six minutes rise onto a track. Go right and keep uphill, past a track off right. Take the second track to the right, which heads downhill and becomes a path leading past a small white church (**1h21min**). The path skirts round this small pastoral valley through the olive groves, back towards the sea, and meets a track four minutes later. Keep ahead down the track for a further four minutes and, as the track swings right, cut off the loop by staying ahead on a path. Rejoin the track and turn left then right at the next junction of tracks soon after.

Immediately on the left now is the continuation of the path (**1h31min**), which becomes more of a sunken trail as you descend in the shade of woods. In eight minutes, turn right on meeting a narrow track, then go right again (**1h46min**). Soon pass a track coming in from the right (Walk 10), as the track levels out across the cultivated plain behind Kokkari. Kokkari's main church, our goal, is now in view. Cross the BYPASS and keep straight on where the track joins a narrow road (**1h53min**). Then take the first right, to emerge on the main road by the church in **Kokkari** two minutes later. This is where the bus stops but, if you have time, continue down to the seafront for a swim.

9 MAVRATZEI TO MYTILINI

See map on reverse of touring map

Distance: 11km/6.8mi; 2h20min

Grade: easy. We start with a section of path, but the walk is mainly on a track, and the ascents are fairly gradual.

Equipment: stout shoes, sunhat, suncream, sunglasses, long trousers or shorts, long-sleeved shirt, cardigan, raingear, picnic, water

How to get there: There are two choices. 🚌 from Samos to Chora (Samos-Pythagorion bus, Timetables 4, 4A; journey time 30min). Frequent daily departures in summer; in winter no Sunday departures. Taxi from Chora to Mavratzei (6km). Or 🚌 from Samos to Pythagorion, where it is often easier to get a taxi; same bus as above. Taxi from Pythagorion to Mavratzei (10km).

To return: 🚌 from Mytilini to Samos (Pythagorion-Samos bus, Timetables 4, 4A; journey time 28min). Frequent daily departures in summer; in winter no Sunday buses.

Short walk: Mavratzei to the church and return: 2.4km/1.5mi; 33min. Grade and equipment as main walk. Follow the main walk to the 17min-point and return the same way.

Yodel if you like, for this walk has all the atmosphere of a good mountain hike. It is a neat deception really, and is achieved by the route taking the line of least resistance. You might not think so when you start by going headlong for the hills but, as the mountains close in, you suddenly find that you are turning away to the east and slipping past all those lovely peaks. Before you start, especially if you find monasteries irresistible, be sure to visit Timiou Stavrou (Holy Cross) which is situated just 2km/1.25mi outside Mavratzei. You pass the monastery as you travel by taxi from Chora, so one option is to alight there and complete the 2km journey on foot (although if you only plan to stay a short time, the taxi driver will wait). Save a little time, too, for wandering around Mavratzei and peeping into the pottery shops.

Head for the small square in the centre of **Mavratzei** and **start the walk** by continuing through it, to leave the village from the north. After **2min** the road reduces to a waymarked trail, more or less as you pass the last house in the village. As you head into the first olive grove, you will find an interesting selection of wild flowers. The first to catch our eye was a rather unusual, all-yellow form of honeywort. Honeywort, or *Cerinthe major,* is a handsome wild flower which graces the roadside and foot paths throughout almost all of Samos. It is easily distinguished by the cylindrical yellow drooping flowers which normally have a rich brown base. And there are always orchids, of course.

In the context of this walk we shall mention but one, the fragrant bug orchid, *Orchis coriophora ssp fragrans,* much in evidence here in May, but less common elsewhere on the island. As the name suggests, this one is sweetly scented, unlike the parent species, the bug orchid, which has a foetid smell not unlike squashed bedbugs (or so we are led to believe).

The trail leads through the olive groves. Ignore a track coming in from the right. Soon you reach a fork (**14min**). The main walk follows the rough track to the right here. Almost immediately, go right along a path. Keep ahead, parallel with the mountains which rise grandly over to the left. The CHURCH shown at the right is reached in **17min**. *(The Short walk turns back here.)*

The waymarked path continues in a gentle ascent up the valley. At a fork where both paths are way-marked (**27min**), go right*; not far above a cement works, you cross a section of old landslip (**35min**) which at present poses no problem for the agile. Join a track in **42min** and continue to the right. Less than one minute along, Walk 10 ascends the track on your left. Route-finding is easy now, since this track takes you virtually all the way to Mytilini. Relax and enjoy the scenery to the full. Just five minutes along the track brings you to a point where you can look back along the route you have just followed and enjoy some fine views down the valley towards Mavratzei and Pagondas. This is just about the highest point of the walk (at 370m/1220ft), and from here the track continues along the top of a ridge for a time — through open pine forest, with views all around. The tracks are glaringly white in this region; keep sunglasses handy.

Leaving the ridge in **1h15min,** the track starts to wind downhill in deep bends, to pass around the head of a valley. There is a very distinct change in the landscape now, as all the dry brightness is replaced by a much softer green. Patches of graceful cypress trees dotting the landscape give the valley a pastoral appeal.

---

*Alternatively, the less agile can fork left, down through olive grove terraces. Turn right on meeting a narrow road and follow it below a cement works, where it reverts to track (30min). Wind uphill for five minutes, to rejoin the main walk at the 42min-point.

This church is reached less than 20min from the start of both Walks 9 and 10. There is a cement works nearby, but it's out of sight.

If you notice the tall purple spathe of the dragon arum, *Dracunculus vulgaris,* which grows on many parts of the island, then get your nose close to the bowl at the bottom of the flower and have a good smell. Isn't it absolutely disgusting? It is as close to the smell of rotting meat as you are likely to encounter any- where, and that is exactly what the flower sets out to imitate. The purpose is to attract flies and, just to make sure, the bowl of the flower actually warms above ambient temperature to give off this irresistible odour. Dozens of flies enter the bowl, where they are trapped by the

Dragon arum

hair structure. But at the end of the same day the pollen is released by the flower to shower down on the flies, the hairs collapse, and the flies escape unharmed to continue to the next flower, which they pollinate in the same way.

You reach a water source (**1h48min**) and, imme- diately afterwards, a sheltered spot at the entrance to the small church of **Ag. Ioannis**. About 1km further on, turn left on a wide track. This track becomes surfaced just before the junction with the Kokkari road/track (**2h**). Turn right at the junction, to head down into **Mytilini** and the bus stop in the centre (**2h20min**).

10 MAVRATZEI TO KOKKARI

See map on reverse of touring map; see also photographs pages 48, 78-79

Distance: 12.6km/7.8mi; 2h56min

Grade: moderate. The ascending part of this walk takes you up to an altitude of around 400m/1300ft, but does so through gradual undulations along footpaths and tracks which are generally good.

Equipment: stout shoes or walking boots, sunhat, suncream, sunglasses, long-sleeved shirt, long trousers, cardigan, raingear, picnic, water; warm hat in early spring

How to get there: There are two choices. 🚌 from Samos to Chora (Samos-Pythagorion bus, Timetables 4, 4A; journey time 30min). Frequent daily departures in summer; in winter no Sunday departures. Taxi from Chora to Mavratzei (6km). *Or* 🚌 from Samos to Pythagorion, where it is often easier to get a taxi; same bus as above. Taxi from Pythagorion to Mavratzei (10km).
To return: 🚌 from Kokkari to Samos (Karlovassi-Samos bus, Timetables 1,1A; journey time 17min). Daily departures in summer. There are often extra buses running from Tsamadou Beach; see footnote to Timetable 1. In winter no Sunday departures.

Alternative walks: The two alternatives suggested below follow the main route for a time and then turn off it, to lead you back to Mytilini. Grade and equipment as for the main walk.

1 Mavratzei — Mytilini: 10.5km/6.5mi; 2h30min. Follow the main walk for 1h19min (the junction with Walk 7), then turn right and walk along the major track to Mytilini (see map; you are following Walk 7 in reverse).

2 Mavratzei — Mytilini: 12.7km/7.9mi; 3h. Follow the main walk to the 1h45min-point. Don't turn left here, but take the track straight ahead along the descending ridge. Keep going until, 45min later, you reach the track which is the route of Walk 8; turn right here and walk on to Mytilini past the reservoir (see map; this is Walk 8 in reverse).

As you slip into that pleasurable mood of relaxation after a full day's walking, helped, no doubt, by the soporific effect of the excellent Samaina wine and the warm night air of the Aegean, it is often a time for reflection and to enjoy again the events of the day. When you think back on this walk, you are sure to wonder why there is such a good sense of adventure. Striking almost directly across the island, the route soon leaves behind all signs of habitation and heads into the wild unknown. You cross isolated areas, streams, and hidden valleys, following the line of a very old path which has long since fallen into disuse. All too soon olive groves appear and you are back walking along a track again, but the sense of isolation is not lost. Continue on by plunging into a remote valley, just below the mountains which hide Kastro Louloudes (Walk 7). You'll spot a huge carob tree in front of a white house at the bottom of this valley. The carob or locust tree, *Ceratonia siliqua,* has been known since antiquity and has a history full of interesting tales, such as its connection with the goldsmith. If there are any seed pods around, break them open to see the uniformity of the seeds: these were used as weights — the original 'carat' of the jewellery trade.

Start out by using the notes for Walk 9 on page 77. At **42min**, when the path joins the track, turn right and look for an ascending track on the left, less than one minute along. As you reach the short ridge, four minutes up this track, you can relax for a moment to enjoy the views. On one side the foothills of the Ambelos range decline in graceful folds to the plains of Mili while, turning to the other side, the valley which we are about to penetrate is headed by rugged mountains.

Continue along the track as it descends the side of the valley. In around 12 minutes the track winds down to an olive grove, where it peters out into a path. Follow the path past a telegraph pole on the right and onto a narrow spur of rock. After a short clamber down over the rock, keep right initially (there is a cave to the left). Although the track below you looks close, there is a big drop here — so head left along the contours of the spur, keeping the track down to your right. This way the track is easily accessed at the point where it makes a horse-shoe bend (**1h06min**). Turn left to continue along the track.

These olive groves, typical of Samos, are met at 1h into the walk.

There is a good resting place at the small white church passed on the left in **1h15min**, but no water. A track junction looms at **1h19min**; make a hairpin bend to the left, joining the route of Walk 7 for a spell. *(But for Alternative walk 1, take the major track to the right here.)* This is the steepest uphill section of the walk, but you soon reach a T-junction of tracks (**1h36min**) where you overlook the north coast. Turn right here (Walk 7 goes left), and head for a cutting in the hill. This is just about the highest point on the walk and, as you pass through the cutting, you are rewarded with extensive views down towards Mytilini and to the south coast.

Around six minutes beyond the cutting (**1h45min**), turn down the track to the left. *(But keep straight ahead for Alternative walk 2.)* Ignore the fork to the left which comes up immediately. Descend the track into a beautiful, once-cultivated valley, where pink oleanders add a splash of colour by the tiny stream. Once over the stream, a gentle climb leads up past a small farm (**2h04min**). Stay left with the main track three minutes later, then turn right at a T-junction in a further two minutes. This soon leads to a five-way junction of tracks (**2h12min**), where Walk 8 comes in from the right. Take the higher, second track to the left. You pass a ramshackle smallholding on the right. When the track sweeps right, cut off a loop by heading down a path through the pines, then continue across the track to cut off a further loop. Turn right on rejoining the track, to meet a diagonal crossing of tracks.* Continue in the same direction, but head across onto the upper track. Kokkari can be seen from time to time through the gaps between the bright yellow bushes of Spanish broom as you descend. Ignore the track coming joining from the left as your track bends to the right.

In **2h35min**, as you round a bend to the left, go sharp right down a woodland track. Keep left on the track, ignoring tracks off right, as it winds down the hillside. As you reach cultivation, Kokkari and its church come into view over to the right. Stay left at the fork in **2h45min** and turn right on meeting the track to Kokkari two minutes later (Walk 8 joins from the left here). Cross the BYPASS and keep ahead as the track joins a road. Take the first road on the right to emerge on the main road in **Kokkari**, by the church and bus stop (**2h56min**).

*From this point you have the option of ending the walk by following Walk 8 (from the 1h11min-point, page 76).

11 CHORA (HORA) • MILI • IREON (HERAION) • PYTHAGORION

Map begins on the reverse of the touring map, ends on page 67

Distance: 20km/12.5mi; 3h55min

Grade: easy-moderate. Only the length raises the grade: this is a mainly-level walk, with only a gentle climb, finishing with a canter round the bay.

Equipment: stout shoes, sunhat, suncream, sunglasses, long trousers or shorts, long-sleeved shirt, cardigan, raingear, picnic, water

How to get there: 🚌 from Samos to Chora (Samos-Mytilini-Pythagorion bus, Timetables 4, 4A; journey time 30min). Frequent daily departures in summer; in winter no Sunday departures.

To return: 🚌 from Pythagorion to Samos (Timetables 4, 4A; journey time 20min or 43min via Mytilini). Frequent daily departures in summer; in winter no Sunday buses.

Shorter walks: There is a good selection of shorter versions or alternatives from which to choose, but most of them are only possible when the summer bus timetable is in operation. All fall into the easy grade, and all require equipment as above.

1 Ireon — Pythagorion: 7km/4.4mi; 1h20min. Take a bus to Ireon (Timetable 7) and walk from there to Pythagorion.

2 Mili — Ireon — Pythagorion: 16km/10mi; 2h45min. Take a taxi from Chora or Pythagorion to Mili and join the main walk at the 1h15min-point.

3 Mili — Ireon: 6.0km/4.3mi; 1h20min. Take a taxi to Mili and follow the main walk from the 1h15min-point to Ireon. Catch a bus from there back to Samos (Timetable 7).

4 Chora — Mili — Ireon: 13.2km/8.25mi; 2h25min. Follow the main walk to Ireon, and return from there to Samos by bus (Timetable 7).

Chora, once the capital of the island, overlooks a cultivated plain where olives and oranges have flourished since ancient times. This is a great walk in spring, when orange blossom perfumes the air. Once at sleepy Ireon, culture vultures can step back in time some 2500 years by visiting the Temple of Hera, one of the wonders of the ancient world. A sacred way connected the temple with Pythagorion, where remains of this earlier capital are constantly being uncovered. If you like your history more natural, the region near Mili is one of the finest on the island for massed displays of flowers. Never before have we seen such huge colonies of the *Serapias,* or tongue orchids, and there are other goodies besides.

Alight from the bus in **Chora** at the junction with the Pyrgos road. **Start the walk** along the road by heading west towards Pyrgos. On reaching the edge of the town (**8min**), take the tarmac road forking down to the left; it eventually reverts to track. The first few kilometres meander gently across the plain through olive and orange groves, towards the low-lying hills which edge the plain. Ahead to the right on the hillside, halfway between Koumaradei and Mili, is the monastery of Megalis Panagias. Although the track divides several times, stay on the major track heading more or less southwest, towards Pagondas nestling on the hillside. Mili comes into view below Pagondas after **43min**.

On reaching **Mili** (**1h12min**), keep ahead on joining the main road on a bend.* Stay ahead as the main road sweeps left, and turn up to the right by the church, to reach the square (**1h15min**), where you can enjoy a simple taverna lunch in a lovely village atmosphere.

Leave the square and head down the road by the church. Turn right and continue until the river is reached in five minutes, by a workshop on the right. Head left here**, to cross the stream bed diagonally to the right, joining a woodland trail. A minute later, the trail crosses another stream bed and starts climbing southwest.

The trail now takes you climbing up the side of a valley in the direction of Pagondas. Oranges give way to olives as you gain higher ground and, very soon (**1h42min**), the trail reaches the road. Turn left here and follow the road downhill. (For those with time and energy to spare; **Pagondas** lies a further 1km along the road to the right, but a detour of only 100m/yds provides a good viewpoint of this large hill village.) Don't get too immersed in the views back towards Mili and the hills beyond, for there is a path on the right to watch for in just 15 minutes. This path immediately joins a track where you keep right. At this point there is a very different vista: the whole of the fertile plain which borders the bay between Ireon and Pythagorion comes into view, as does a glimpse of Turkey beyond, and Sarakini's Tower below.

*Flower-lovers: turn right here, then take the second track off to the right, by a signpost to Koumaradei and Megalo Panagia. A detour down this track takes you across slightly swampy fields to some huge colonies of the tongue orchids mentioned above. This is also one of two areas on the island where you can see the tall graceful spikes of the purple *Orchis laxiflora.* There is a rather pretty *Allium,* too, *Allium roseum.* (Allow 40 minutes return.)

**At about the 1h22min-point, you *may* find fallen trees still blocking the trail: in this case, return to the workshop and turn sharp left. In less than six minutes, turn sharp left down another track, to cross the valley floor. This track rises to meet the trail from Mili in nine minutes. Turn right uphill to continue.

Continue ahead now, as you start to descend through sparse pine woods and, when you reach a junction in **2h12min**, turn right. Stay with the track as it bends around to the left, and keep left as tracks join from the right. When a road is reached (**2h25min**), turn right to head directly into **Ireon**. Cross the first road, and head for the second road behind the shore. (The bus stops on the right here, between the two roads.) Turn left along the shore road and, on the edge of Ireon, immediately after crossing a bridge, turn right down a track towards the sea (or stay on the road, if you want to visit the Temple of Hera; from the temple you can later walk on to the beach).

Now just follow the beach all the way around the bay to Pythagorion. Leave the beach to join the road as you come into **Pythagorion** (map page 67) and continue ahead to the bus stop (**3h55min**). If you have time, there are more ancient remains to inspect, or go down to the quayside and enjoy the ambience.

Quay at Ireon

12 PANDROSOS • PROFITIS ILIAS • MANOLATES • PLATANAKIA

Map on reverse of touring map; see also photos pages 21, 25, 91

Distance: 18.5km/11.5mi; 4h

Grade: strenuous, but not as difficult as it might seem. Pandrosos is situated at an elevation of around 600m/2000ft, which only leaves some 540m/1800ft to climb to reach the highest point — and at the start of the walk, while you are still fresh.

Equipment: walking boots, sunhat, suncream, sunglasses, long trousers, long-sleeved shirt, cardigan, compass, picnic, water; outside high summer warm clothing, including woollen hat and gloves

How to get there: 🚌 from Samos to Pyrgos (Samos-Karlovassi bus, inland route, Timetable 2; journey time 1h). Departures weekdays only, summer and winter. Taxi from Pyrgos to Pandrosos (6km).
To return: 🚌 from Platanakia to (Samos Karlovassi-Samos bus, coastal route, Timetables 1, 1A; journey time 25min). Departures daily in summer, weekdays only in winter.

Shorter walk: Pandrosos — Pyrgos: 10.4km/6.5mi; 2h30min; moderate; equipment as above. Follow the start of the main walk, climbing up the path and track from Pandrosos, until the main track is reached in 42min. From this high vantage point (950m/3120ft) you can enjoy some fine views down to the south as you turn left to wander down the track, ignoring any side tracks, to emerge just outside Pandrosos. Turn right here and continue down to Pyrgos on the road. Return to Samos by bus (Karlovassi-Samos bus, inland route, Timetable 2; journey time 1h). Departures weekdays only, year round.

Alternative walk: Pandrosos — Profitis Ilias — Pandrosos — Pyrgos: 15km/9.3mi; 3h30min; grade and equipment as main walk. Follow the main walk to reach the summit of Profitis Ilias in 1h20min and then return by the same route, but follow the track all the way down (as in the Shorter walk above), to reach first Pandrosos in 2h30min, and then Pyrgos 1h later. Return by bus as in the Shorter walk.

This walk crosses the entire Ambelos range from south to north, via the highest point, Profitis Ilias (1140m/ 3740ft). Tackling these high mountain walks always fills us with a delicious sense of anticipation. Morphologically, the summit of Profitis Ilias disappoints, for it is nothing more than a large, almost flatish lump. But its views are magnificent. The eastern side of the island is laid out before you like a map while, over to the west, the eyes are irresistibly drawn to the huge rocky ridge which dominates the Kerkis range. Vigla, the highest peak (1440m/4725ft; Walk 16), is at the southern end of this ridge. The real pleasure of this hike is that you spend so much time walking at high altitude (around 1000m/3300ft), through vegetation of great botanical interest. We made many exciting discoveries, including snow-drops and crocuses at Eastertime, the rather special yellow fritillary, *Fritillaria bithynica,* which has such a limited distribution and, of course, orchids. Two species which are common here, but hard to find elsewhere, are *Orchis mascula ssp pinetorum* (closely related to the European early purple orchid, but notice how robust these specimens are) and *Dactylorhiza romana,* which occurs in two colour forms, pink and yellow. We know of nowhere else where you can actually see both colours, and all shades in between, at the same time. See also Walk 13 for notes about the flowers of this region.

Walk up into **Pandrosos** from where the taxi drops passengers. Pass through a square (seasonal taverna, but

Terraces dominate the landscape on the descent from Manolates to Platanakia. Vourliotes lies beyond the ridge in the background.

no bread shop), to a higher square. **The walk starts** here (with the yellow-painted church shown on page 21 in the far right-hand corner as you enter). Immediately you enter this square, turn left into the waymarked street which heads left at first, then uphill to the right. It reduces to a waymarked path above the village. Ignore the strong waymarked path forking left (**5min**); keep straight ahead, following the stream bed for about 10m/yds, then turn up to the right. In **11min** keep left with the waymarks (where the main path appears to go straight on). All this early section is a good steady climb through *macchie,* but once under way the path is easy to follow.

In **16min** the path becomes a track and rises up onto a woodland track a minute later: turn right. The path continues less than a minute later, when the track ends, but be careful to follow the waymarked path up to the left. When the path meets a track (**32min**), turn left. Keep up on this track, ignoring a minor crossing track, to reach a major track 10 minutes later (by a fenced vineyard on the right; **42min**). Turn right. *(The Shorter walk goes left here.)* Head uphill on this track for 15 minutes, then fork left (**57min**) up a distinct track, which *may* be signposted to Profitis Ilias. *(Walk 13 goes straight ahead at this point.)* For the final assault, follow this track, but look for the waymarked path going straight ahead on the first bend; it rejoins the track higher up. Turn right and strike out over the stony and barren ground to the church at the SUMMIT OF **Profitis Ilias** (**1h20min**).

Once you have enjoyed the views and satisfied your curiosity about the two structures by the church, we can get under way again. Leave from behind the church (on

The old-style ovens are still to be seen dotted about the island but they are now only used at Eastertime. Lamb is the traditional fare throughout Greece for this celebration, but Samos has its own speciality — oven-roasted goat, with a rice stuffing. Spit-roasting of the goat is a popular alternative, and the 4-5 hours of continuous hand-turning is just part of the fun, with quite a lot of retsina being consumed.

a compass bearing of 340°) and, in less than two minutes, look for a red arrow and waymarks which will take you down the right side and off the summit. These marks, which cover only a short section, are easily seen on the ascent, but difficult to find going downhill. Once off the hump, the path leads round to the left, onto a lightly-wooded saddle. Cross this to another hump — a mini version of the main summit. Climb this hill, but keep over to the left and continue round the left side, until you see a track below you. Make your way down to join the track (**1h35min**) and turn right. Now you can enjoy some fairly easy, almost level walking. Turn right at the track junction reached in **1h55min** and continue along here for 13 minutes, until another track junction is reached, where you again turn right. It's almost time to leave the track section of the walk behind so, six minutes from the last junction (**2h14min**), take the track off left, which leads to and skirts above a vineyard. A few minutes along the track, as it swings right in the direction of Manolates, a foray up left, to the right of a prominent rocky outcrop, leads to a delightful picnic spot with good views down to the coast. Return to the track and, when it ends (**2h19min**), continue on the waymarked path down to Manolates. The descent gives an ever-changing vista along the north coast; at times you can even see Nissi beyond Samos town. The path is obvious for most of the way, but do keep your eyes on the waymarks.

In **3h09min**, on reaching a junction of paths, turn left to enter **Manolates**, by the fountain, just four minutes later. Although this is a rather sleepy hill village, some tavernas stay open through the afternoon siesta. To leave Manolates just wander through the village and join the road at the lower end. Follow the road out and, in **3h28min**, descend the steps to the right, to join a path. A farm track cuts across it just five minutes along: turn right and look carefully for your ongoing track, on the left, in under three minutes (just before a small house on the right). Two minutes down the track, just before a church, turn right on a path. It takes you back to the old trail down to the left. In **3h45min** you meet the road in the Valley of the Nightingales. Cross the bridge ahead (near the setting shown on page 25), and turn right, down to **Platanakia** (**4h**). The bus stops just where you arrive back on the coast road, and there is good drinking water on tap there, too.

13 PANDROSOS • LAZARUS • KOKKARI

See map on reverse of touring map; see also photos pages 21, 48

Distance: 17.2km/10.7mi; 4h25min

Grade: strenuous, but not as difficult as it might seem. We start at 600m/2000ft, leaving only around 550m/1800ft of climbing, most of it during the early section of the walk, while you are still fresh.

Equipment: walking boots, sunhat, suncream, sunglasses, long trousers, long-sleeved shirt, cardigan, picnic, water; warm clothing, including woollen hat and gloves, outside high summer

How to get there: 🚌 from Samos to Pyrgos (Samos-Karlovassi bus, inland route, Timetable 2; journey time 1h). Departures weekdays only (summer and winter). Taxi from Pyrgos to Pandrosos (6km).
To return: 🚌 from Kokkari (Karlovassi-Samos bus, coastal route, Timetables 1,1A; journey time 20min). No Sunday departures in winter.

Shorter walk: Pandrosos — Kokkari: 16.7km/10.4mi; 3h55min. You can omit the summit of Lazarus, but the walk is still strenuous and requires equipment as above. The route to the summit is simply a diversion which returns you to the same point on the track, so just ignore that section of the instructions.

Alternative walks: same grade and equipment as the main walk

1 Pandrosos — Profitis Ilias — Lazarus — Kokkari: 19.2km/12mi; 5h10min. If you do not have time to do Walk 12, you can include Profitis Ilias in this walk. Follow Walk 12 to the top of Profitis Ilias, then retrace your steps back to the track you left at the 57min-point and continue.

2 Pandrosos — Lazarus — Kokkari: 17km/10.5mi; 4h50min. You can walk to Kokkari by following Walks 7 and 10. At the 2h58min-point, turn right along the track instead of keeping ahead to the church. Then follow Walk 7 in reverse for 33min, by referring to the map. When you arrive at the track going down to the right (the route of Walk 10), keep ahead to a cutting in the hill. Now follow Walk 10 from just after the 1h36min-point (page 82).

3 Pandrosos — Lazarus — Moni Vronda — Kokkari: 17.5km/10.9mi; 5h. At the 2h58min point turn left along the track. Use the map to descend to Moni Vronda (which is in view). From there follow Walk 1 from the 1h22min-point (page 47), to descend to Kokkari.

In scenery and vegetation this walk is worlds apart from nearby Walk 12. Soil conditions and perhaps accessibility favour cultivation; thus you'll see vine-yards everywhere, reaching up to heights of 1000m/3300ft. If you are up there very early in the day, then you can witness the 'rush hour' of workers going up to the vineyards. We return to the heights again; this time tackling Lazarus, the third highest peak in the Ambelos range, standing at an elevation of 1025m/3360ft. It is a peak full of character, with a shape so distinctive that it is a landmark visible for miles around and is clearly seen from Samos town: look for the peak which has a long sloping flank to the east and a steep face to the

Terraces below Pandrosos (Walks 12 and 13)

west (photograph pages 54-55). Below, to the north, is a much smaller peak with a similar shape know as Lasaraki or 'Little Lazarus'. Finding the wild paeony shown on page 124, *Paeonia mascula,* gave us a lot of pleasure, as did some large colonies of the toothed orchid, *Orchis tridentata.* The latter find was particularly pleasing, since there had previously been only one uncertain sighting of this species on Samos.

Start out from the square in **Pandrosos**. Follow Walk 12 to the point where the track forks left to the summit of Profitis Ilias (**57min**). Keep straight on here. *(Or go up to the summit of Profitis Ilias and return to this point for Alternative walk 1.)* In four minutes rise up to a high point, then start to descend. From here the views change and, suddenly, you can see as far as Samos town: the harbour is clearly visible. Go sharp left down a track (**1h09min**)*; it reduces to a path a minute later. (This area is sometimes used as a temporary goatherds' camp.) The looming mass of Lazarus, ahead to the right, is a good landmark, as the path more or less heads in that direction. Keep uphill past some water seepage (where the path is vague), to walk in front of a large plane tree (**1h14min**). Two minutes later, cross a low stone retaining wall (which serves as a water trough in winter), below another large plane tree. Keep slightly uphill, rising onto a grassy area (**1h20min**), with the peak of Lazarus ahead. Although the path can

*This route requires some path-finding skills; as an alternative, you can stay ahead on the main track, rejoining the walk at the 1h33min-point.

The mastic tree, Pistacia lentiscus, *can be seen on many walks. Refresh yourself by smelling the crushed leaf, for this is the species which has been domesticated on the nearby island of Chios for the production of gum,* mastica, *which is used in the making of sweets. It's a most refreshing flavour. If you want to try the sweets, head for the local cake shop* (zaxeroplasteion) *and ask for mastica sweets.*

be vague at times, there are some old red waymarks which help. Start into a gradual descent and emerge in a meadow. Ignore paths leading upwards, and head across the meadow, to locate your ongoing descending path. (Do not be tempted to go down sharply right towards the track below; the path descends gently along the rock-strewn hillside.) When you emerge on a bend of the track (**1h33min**), turn left uphill.

Lazarus now looms ever larger over to your right and, in **1h45min**, you reach the point where you divert to the summit. *(But keep straight on for the Shorter walk.)* As you walk by the steep western face of Lazarus (but *before* the track starts to turn away to the left), look for the path going off to the right and follow it. It leads you through the trees to a clearing in under a minute. Here turn sharp left, following the edge of the clearing and heading directly for the base of the western face. A large red cross, painted on a rock facing you, marks the start of a zigzag path leading to the stony summit. It takes just 15 minutes to reach the SUMMIT OF **Lazarus** (**2h**). There are some fine views to be enjoyed from up here, but the remains of a hill fort may especially capture your attention. These look very similar to Kastro Louloudes (Walk 7), which means that they probably date back to the 14th or 15th century, to the time when people were driven from the island by plundering. The few who remained took refuge in these hill forts, where they lived an isolated existence for almost a hundred years.

Return from the summit by the same route, to rejoin the track (**2h15min**). In one minute, as the track sweeps left, go down the path on the right. This stony path takes you through sparse woodland*, to a track (**2h27min**). Turn right but, in under two minutes (beyond a water source on the left), fork up the track to the right. Soon, as you approach a ruin, fork left on a rough track. This

---

*Should fallen trees block the path half way down, skirt round them to the left. The path runs roughly in a westerly direction.

reverts to path and contours the hillside with views towards Kokkari through the trees. At a fork (**2h33min**), turn right, down into the woods. (Or first keep ahead two minutes to **Lazaraki**. A short climb leads to tremendous views.)

The waymarked path forks down to the left in five minutes and dips down over a small gully three minutes later. Descend onto a narrow saddle (**2h49min**) and continue left down the path, which becomes a sunken trail. Be sure to take a steep path down left five minutes later, following it carefully to a rough track. On meeting further tracks, turn right, left, and right again. Almost immediately after this second right turn, take the path diagonally down to the left, to reach the main track (**2h58min**). Cross the track and head for the small church of **Ag. Dimitrios**, enjoying views of Moni Vronda over to the left. *(But turn right on the track here for Alternative walk 2 and left for Alternative walk 3.)*

Locate the waymarked path at the right of the church. This descends past a huge plane tree and then along the edge of terraces. Follow the waymarks carefully as you leave the terraces and descend to the stream bed on the right (**3h04min**). Cross and continue down the far side, to come to a shallow stepped meadow two minutes later. Keep ahead initially, then edge over to the track on the left a minute later. Turn right on the track and, after it swings left towards Moni Vronda, take a path off right (just past a shallow dip that looks like the start of a field track; **3h09min**). Some waymarks appear; follow these closely, as the path is vague at first. You are heading for the right-hand edge of the limestone scar ahead, but this is lost to view as you descend through pine woods. You emerge close to the limestone scar and wind down to meet the track from Moni Vronda (**3h 26min**). Now follow Walk 1 from the 1h 55min-point (page 48) to descend to **Kokkari** (**4h25min**).

Ag. Dimitrios

14 PLATANOS • KONDEIKA • YDROUSSA • KONDAKEIKA • AG. DIMITRIOS OR KARLOVASSI

Distance: 15km/9.3mi; 3h11min to *Ag. Dimitrios;* 17.6km/11mi; 4h to *Karlovassi*

Grade: moderate. There is not too much uphill walking, although we do start with a climb of 150m/500ft. The normal ups and downs follow, but usually on tracks and paths which are good underfoot.

Equipment: stout shoes or walking boots, sunhat, suncream, sunglasses, long-sleeved shirt, long trousers, cardigan, raingear, picnic, water

How to get there: 🚍 (or taxi) from Samos to the Platanos road junction (Samos-Karlovassi bus, inland route, Timetable 2; journey time 1h25min). Departures weekdays only, summer and winter. Alternatively (or on weekends) take the Samos-Karlovassi bus along the coastal route (timetables 1, 1A) and a taxi for the 10km journey to the Platanos road junction or up to Platanos.
To return: 🚍 from Ag. Dimitrios or Karlovassi to Samos (Karlovassi-Samos bus, coastal route, Timetables 1, 1A; journey time 50min-1h). Daily departures in summer; in winter there are no suitable buses on Sundays.

Short walk: Both start at Ydroussa, the 1h52min-point in the main walk, and both require equipment as above. Only the summer bus timetables are suitable; otherwise take a taxi to start. Take the Samos-Karlovassi bus via the coastal route (Timetables 1, 1A) and then the bus from Karlovassi to Ydroussa (Timetable 8).

1 Ydroussa — Ag Dimitrios (6.5km/4mi; 1h20min) **or Karlovassi** (7.7km/4.8mi; 2h); easy. Follow the main walk from Ydroussa.

2 Ydroussa — Platanos road junction: 8.7km/5.5mi; 1h50min; easy. Follow the main walk in reverse by referring to the map, and catch the early afternoon bus for Samos (Timetable 2).

It was on this walk that we learnt the art of passing a donkey tethered on a narrow path. Our instructor was a young girl who gave a faultless demonstration and made it look as easy as it should be. All you do is approach unhurriedly, pick up the tether rope and pull it gently towards you. The donkey responds by trotting past you; it is as easy as that. As you walk along the high-level road between Platanos and Kondeika, a breathtaking panorama opens up the very moment you can see from coast to coast from Karlovassi to Ormos Marathokambos. Onto this canvas a master artist has brushed in the whole of the Kerkis range. Raise your camera, as you surely will, but somehow the grandeur of this scenery defies capture as a mere photographic image. And it is the same with Petaloudes, a little-known beauty spot encountered later in the walk; but this time it is the intimacy of the place which eludes a good photographic angle. Huge plane trees dwarf the already-tiny white church. As always, there is plenty of botanical interest, but look out for one Samos speciality in particular: the small, bristly-haired shrub with blue long-tubed flowers called *Lithodora hispidula*. It grows in a number of places on the island, but seems to be especially common around Ydroussa. It has such a limited geographical distribution (being found elsewhere only on Crete, Karpathos and Rhodes), that it is worth seeing while you have the chance.

Alight from the bus at the **Platanos** ROAD JUNCTION and **start the walk** by heading up the road to Platanos. After only **2min** take the old trail leading off to the right (just past a track on the right). When the trail is interrupted by the road, the continuation is usually just a few paces to the right but, when you emerge on the road in **13min**, you must turn right along it, round a bend, and then look for the waymarked trail on the right a full minute later. Already the views of the Kerkis range are impressive as you reach higher ground, and they improve once you have turned left on rejoining the road

Peta-loudes, an enchanting glade (Picnic 14)

(**18min**) and are walking the final stretch into Platanos. The village square at **Platanos**, with its *kafeneions,* is reached in **21min**. Cross the square, and leave by the Kondeika road on the left. Magnificent views more than compensate for this stretch of road walking. Cut off two loops in the road by keeping ahead on a rough track (at **35min** and again at **44min**).

As you enter **Kondeika** in **54min**, passing the church on the left, turn right to keep the village square on your left. Continue downhill on this road and look out within two minutes for a cobbled trail on your left, marked by a red arrow. Descend this trail, which is very stony in places. Then continue along track, past a building on the right. Skirting a vineyard (**1h02min**), you meet another track four minutes later. Turn right and head down towards a stream in the valley floor (**1h15min**).

Cross the stream diagonally, to ascend the track opposite. In three minutes, on coming to a junction with a plane tree, go left. Keep on the main track, ignoring tracks off left and right. At **1h36min**, when the main track swings left at a junction, turn right (there are large metal gates on the left). Follow the track in a bend to the left. Rise up, ignoring tracks off to the right. As the track starts to descend and curve around to the left, keep straight ahead on a waymarked path. The path remains at a sufficient elevation to give pleasing views as you pass through the open areas. At **1h42min** keep right on a woodland track. When you meet the concrete road five minutes later, turn right to **Ydroussa**. Head into the village, then wend your way past *kafeneions,* down to the large *platea* by the main church (**1h52min**).

Leave Ydroussa by heading back uphill from the main *platea* to the northeastern corner. Head left along Odos Kapetan Laxana, then go right on a track (it is concreted at the outset). Continue round the contours of the hill, ignoring a track off to the right seven minutes along. At a distinct fork, where the main track sweeps right (**2h13min**), descend to the left on a rough track (a water pipe runs beneath the entrance to this track). You descend to cross a stream bed a minute later. Watch for waymarks and turn left into the woods (**2h16min**), to arrive at **Petaloudes** (Picnic 14) a minute later. When you have recovered from your surprise and delight at this beautiful glade, take a minute to see the fine old frescoes inside the church.

Leave Petaloudes by following the track from the

Ag. Nikolaos

Samos →

Ag. Dimitrios

17-21
114-115

Karlovassi

8

14

Kondakeika

14

100

200

400

14

Petaloudes

14

Neo
Karlovassi

100

100

200

Ydroussa

14

14

100

200

400

300

Sourides

200

Kondeika

100

300

14

400

Ag.
Theodori

300

14

500

400

Platanos

600

300

400

14 →

14

300

600

← Ormos
Marathokambos

Pyrgos

N

0   2 km

1 mi

Koumeika

15
100-101

water source. In three minutes, rejoin the main track by a white pumping station and keep ahead. Just after passing a track joining from the left (by a church), turn right down a way-marked path (**2h24min**). In **2h32min** you meet another track: turn right. Ignore tracks off to the left but, five minutes along, take a waymarked path off to the left (off a bend in the track). Passing through the woods, you might just spot some well-coloured specimens of the broad-leaved *Epipactis helleborine,* which persist in flower well into June.

Turn left when you meet a track (**2h46min**) and follow it into **Kondakeika** (**2h57min**). Go straight through the village, keeping left at the end of it. You meet a narrow crossing road and open views. Turn left to a small *platea.* Cross the *platea* and head down a concrete trail to the right on the far side (beware the steep drop to the right at the bottom of the trail). You have two choices now: either go right to meet the road on a bend and continue down to **Ag. Dimitrios** and the bus (20 minutes; **3h11min**) or walk to Karlovassi (one hour away).

To walk to Karlovassi, keep straight ahead to continue on the concrete trail here. You soon meet a road, where you go left. The road reverts to track by a church on the right (**3h11min**). Two minutes later, pass another church on the left, as the track rises to a T-junction (**3h18min**). Go left, then stay with the main track as it sweeps right to descend to the Ydroussa road (**3h29min**). Turn right and, shortly (as you pass a church on the right), find a path on the left down to the river (**3h31min**).

Cross the river and reach a road. Turn left towards a house with a tall chimney (both currently white). Pass in front of this house and along the left-hand side of it, walking in a shallow concrete irrigation ditch (usually dry). Keep ahead on a field track, heading towards a church. On coming to a road by the church, head right towards Karlovassi.* Eight minutes along the road from the church (not far past a track on the left signposted to Ag. Triada and a shrine), take the next track left. Follow this uphill for 10 minutes, to meet a further track behind a building on the right. Turn right towards a church, but take the path down left before the church is reached. At a junction in four minutes, continue down to the right. Meeting a bend in the road, descend past **Karlovassi** hospital, then keep round left to the bus stop (**4h**).

*You can, of course, just follow the road from here all the way to Karlovassi.

15 KOUTSI • NEOCHORI • KOUMEIKA (BALOS) • ORMOS MARATHOKAMBOS

See photographs pages 1, 41   **Distance:** 11.2km/7mi; 2h25min

Grade: easy-moderate. This is mainly downhill walking; only the loose stony descent to the seashore, which requires some agility, raises the walk from the easy category.

Equipment: sturdy boots, long trousers, long-sleeved shirt, sunhat, suncream, sunglasses, raingear, picnic, water

How to get there: 🚌 from Samos to Koutsi (Kutsi) (Samos-Karlovassi bus via Pyrgos; Timetable 2; journey time 1h05min). Weekdays only. Alternatively: 🚌 from Samos to Karlovassi (Timetables 1, 1A; journey time 1h) or 🚌 from Samos to Marathokambos (Timetable 3). No Sunday buses in winter. Then taxi from Karlovassi or Marathokambos to Koutsi.
To return: 🚌 from Ormos Marathokambos (Timetable 3). Weekdays only in winter. Or 🚌 from Marathokambos (Timetable 3). No Sunday buses in winter. There are taxis at Ormos Marathokambos in summer; otherwise telephone for a taxi or walk up the old route to Marathokambos see description in the box on page 127).

Short walk: Koutsi — Balos: 9km/5.6mi; 1h50min; easy. Equipment as above. Out of high season, arrange in advance for a taxi from Balos. No facilities out of season. At the 1h20min-point, turn left and follow the road down to Balos.

Here is an opportunity to sample some of the southern Samos mountain scenery along an old route to Neochori and Koumeika. Koutsi (Kutsi), where the walk begins, is just an isolated taverna/restaurant by a tumbling stream. It makes a refreshing summer haven, its terraces cooled by many plane trees. Gentle downhill walking leads us past gorges and through some beautiful pastoral scenery, to the sleepy village of Neochori. Forest fires have denuded much of the countryside around Koumeika, but the open views more than compensate. Kerkis dominates the landscape and provides a magnificent backdrop as the walk moves closer to the sea. Just a small hamlet with a tamarisk-backed shingle beach, peaceful Balos makes a relaxing end to the Short walk — a soporific setting for a lunch in the taverna when it opens for the season.

Start the walk along the road above **Koutsi** (Kutsi), by heading west towards Marathokambos. In less than **6min** go left, towards the small church. Just before the church is reached, turn left again, to descend a track. This track initially heads back in the direction of Koutsi, then swings round back towards Marathokambos. When the concrete ends (**10min**), keep ahead on a very stony waymarked path with metal water pipes running alongside. Stay with the water pipes two minutes later, ignoring the fork to the left. Savour the

99

views along this section of the walk, where the path at times reverts to a cobbled trail. Keep ahead and cross a concrete track (**20min**), then pass a shady water source (**23min**). As the trail heads right, up to the village, it is joined by another trail coming from the left. Reach the village square in **Neochori** (**29min**), where a diversion to the right leads to the car park and a superb vantage point over the countryside.

From the square continue ahead through the village (follow red dots on telegraph poles). In two minutes you descend to a small *platea* below the church. Go right here, down the concrete road with a central water channel. The road soon reverts to a trail. The sea comes into view, and then Koumeika. When the trail swings sharply down to the left three minutes later, keep ahead on a small path along the top of a terrace. After leading through olive groves, the path descends left, to a concrete road (**40min**). Turn right uphill for about three minutes, then go left down a rough track (red arrow on the ground). Stay on this track which gradually descends through olive groves towards Koumeika. The olive trees are left behind as the track bends left and meets the road (**59min**), where you turn right. Follow this usually quiet road towards Koumeika. Ignore a first white church on the left (**1h08min**). But go sharp left up an old trail two minutes later, towards the small church above. You rise up to reach the road on the outskirts of Koumeika in a further three minutes. Keep ahead to reach the *platea* in the centre (**1h16min**).

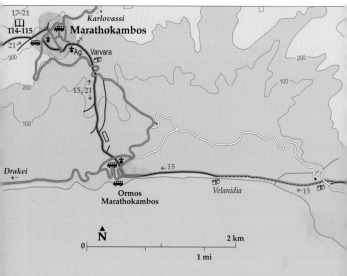

A shaded haven, cooled by the sound of running water from a decorative marble fountain, **Koumeika** *platea* has its share of café/bars, but do not expect anything more substantial than a snack. Leave the *platea* by walking up the narrow village road immediately to the left of the fountain, then keep round to the left. Cross the tarmac road four minutes later (photograph page 1), joining a roughly-concreted track. *(But turn left down the road here for the Short walk to Balos.)* Ignore the track down to the left just after the concrete ends and the track becomes stony. Keep ahead on the main track in the direction of the Kerkis Mountains, which loom ever closer (photograph page 41), and enjoy fine views along the coast from Ormos Marathokambos to Kambos and beyond. At a distinct fork (**1h33min**), go left down a very rough track. Four minutes later, as the track swings left to descend to the track/road, keep ahead on a path. On meeting the track/road in a further two minutes, turn right, then almost immediately left, to continue along the path. Stay on this path, which heads diagonally towards the sea; you pass a house and goat pens on the right. The path has now become a rough stony track and care is needed as it descends steeply to the shore (**1h52min**).

Continue right along the stony shore past the first few summer houses, then rise up to walk more easily along the back of the shore. Enter **Ormos Marathokambos** and head for the far end (**2h25min**). The bus stops on the main road at the top of the steps ahead.

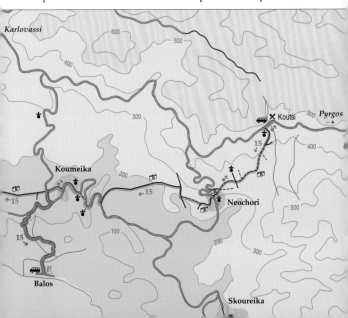

16 VOTSALAKIA (KAMBOS) • MONI EVANGELISTRIA • VIGLA • VOTSALAKIA (KAMBOS)

Distance: 21km/13mi; 6h30min

Grade: very strenuous; only for very fit and experienced walkers. The ascent on this walk is 1440m/4725ft, and almost all of it is on a steep gradient and over very rocky terrain. The summit is often shrouded in cloud, particularly through spring and autumn, so wait until you are enjoying a spell of settled fine weather before you attempt this walk, and **never** attempt it in changeable weather conditions. Be prepared, too, for the wind chill factor on the summit.

Equipment: *compass,* walking boots, long sleeved shirt, long trousers, cardigan, sunhat, suncream, sunglasses, waterproofs, picnic, plenty of water. Warmer clothing is required for spring and autumn.

How to get there: Since an early start is essential for this walk, there are no convenient buses for a one-day excursion. The options are:
1 🚌 from Samos to Votsalakia on the previous day and stay overnight (Samos-Karlovassi-Votsalakia bus; Timetables 3, 3A; journey time 2h). Weekday departures only, summer and winter. *Return* on the same bus.
2 Take an early taxi for the 80km journey to Votsalakia; this is most economical if there is a party of four. *Return* by bus as (1) above.
3 Use a hire car.

Short walk: Votsalakia — Moni Evangelistria — Votsalakia: 10.5km/6.5mi; 2h50min; strenuous. Walk just to the monastery, Evangelistria, and return by the same route. Since the monastery is perched up at 690m/2275ft, this is still a tough walk, but well worth doing for the fine views. Equipment as for the main walk.

Since you have to climb every single inch of the way from sea level, this is a tough route up Vigla, the highest point in the Kerkis range. But there are compensations: it is very direct and certainly the most scenic route we found. There is one other advantage, too: the route is way-marked for most of the way. The monastery, Evangelistria, provides a very convenient halfway resting stage, where you can recharge your water bottles. The nuns might even invite you to partake of a welcoming ouzo ... at 7 in the morning! Not far from the summit, at an elevation of 1160m/3800ft, there is a chapel but, alas, no water. Here, too, is where the waymarking ends, but stay with us, and we will guide you the rest of the way. An early start is recommended on this walk if you want to beat the heat of the day. For us the experience of walking through

Mounds of smouldering charcoal: the controlled combustion of wood to charcoal is a slow process which may take several weeks to complete. This old skill is unlikely to die out, since almost every taverna on the island uses a charcoal grill.

the dawn, and the sunrise itself, is so beautiful that it is etched vividly in our memories. At first there is barely a hint of dawn. The pool of light thrown by the torch guides our footsteps along the rough track, but very soon the edge of a new day pushing over the horizon brightens the sky and lightens the way. There is a cheerful and lively greeting from the birds as the world begins to stir about us and a smell of wood smoke awakens the senses. Nearby, the charcoal man may be just rising from his camp bed to tend the slowly-smouldering mound. Sunrise bathes the mountain in an orange light, and offshore the Fourni Islands float magically in a wash of colour where the orange flows into blue. All too quickly the sun is up, bright and hot, and we give it a silent thanks for persuading us early from our beds and giving us such lasting memories.

One final word: ***leave plenty of time for this walk.*** *Our overall time to reach the top, including breakfast and all other stops, was just **five hours.***

Start out from the bus stop at the western edge of **Votsalakia**, opposite the Hotel Votsalakia. With the sea on your left, follow the road to a track on the right (signposted in Greek to Evangelistria), just after crossing a small bridge (**5min**). Just a minute down this wide track you reach a junction, where you turn left. It seems now as if you are heading for a sheer rock face as you continue along this gently-rising track, but three left turns steer you around it. The first is by the charcoal burner's place, reached in **20min**. The second is at a T-junction two minutes later, and the third two minutes further on. Stay with the track as it winds up through olive groves and keep right at a fork (**30min**). In **38min**

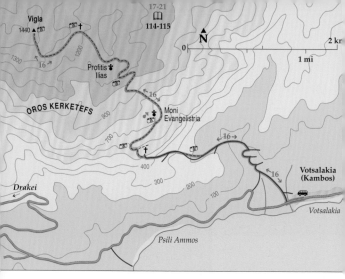

look for a red arrow on a rock on the right; this marks the start of a waymarked section of path. Rejoin the track in **44min** and continue up to the right. Fork right in **58min**, to reach a blue-capped shrine two minutes later, as the track ends. Continue up the path to the left, before the shrine, to a T of paths. Turn left to reach an ideal picnic spot (**1h08min**), with remarkable views out to the Fourni Islands and beautiful Limnionas Bay.

As views open up again to the left (**1h11min**), you enter the grounds of **Moni Evangelistria**, reached in **1h36min**. Rest here for a while, and enjoy some of the sweetest water on Samos. Then leave the monastery by following the path behind the building which heads diagonally right uphill, through pines. Watch out now for a new set of waymarkings in *blue*, both crosses and arrows, painted on trees and rocks. In spite of the large size of the waymarks, concentration is needed to stay on the path, particularly in this wooded section.

The monastery grounds are left behind (**2h**) as the pine woods start to thin and the tree line is approached at an altitude of 875m/2870ft. For a while the path here follows what remains of the vegetative cover, passing through patches of holly oak, before reaching the barren rock. At least the waymarks stand out clearly on the bare rocks, and they are easily followed. Every footstep from here to the summit seems to disturb a thousand grasshoppers.

The next landmark is the chapel of **Profitis Ilias**, reached in **2h45min**. The summit is not too far away now, but there is still some work to do to get there.

Head up, passing to the right of the chapel, and making for the ridge. From there you have a clear view of Vigla directly opposite, identified by the trig point on top. But the valley in front of you is deep enough to warrant a detour: take the path off to the right. It descends slightly, while heading for the scrub-covered double-mounded ridge at its head. Once there, bear left across the first mound (you might just notice a small shrine on top) and skirt the second. From this point Vigla lies over to the left, but you can no longer see it because of the smaller 'false summit' between you and the peak. Head to the right of this smaller summit, choosing one of the many animal tracks, and taking an incline which will lead you gradually upwards as you pass round the mountain.

Vigla comes into view again as you round this false summit, and all that remains now is to head for the base of the sloping left flank of the true summit, then pick your way carefully over the very rocky terrain until the trig point is reached (1440m/4725ft; **3h 30min**). From the windbreak here on Vigla you can enjoy splendid views of the Fourni Islands and of Ikaria beyond, as well as several parts of the Turkish mainland. On Samos some peaks of the Ambelos range can be seen floating above the heat haze in the valleys, creating quite a spectacular effect.

To descend from the summit, return to the chapel and be sure to pick up the blue waymarks again. The sense of elation on completing this memorable walk (**6h30min**) does much to dispel your tiredness.

We pick up many recipes on Samos, and one of our favourites involves the asparagus mentioned in Walk 8. It is hard to imagine that this spiny green scrambling shrub can be eaten, but it is only the soft young shoots produced in the spring that are used. It took no persuasion at all when a Greek friend asked us to go out collecting wild asparagus with him on one occasion. In no time we were back home with a huge armful of shoots, getting the cooking pots ready. Discarding the water, following a short five-minute boil, is the way to remove the bitterness. After the asparagus has been drained, it is tossed into a frying pan with the olive oil already warmed and the onions softened. In just about an ouzo later, a couple of eggs are thrown in to bind everything together — a really appetising meal.

17 KARLOVASSI • PALEO KARLOVASSI • KASTRO • POTAMI • TSOURLEI • PALEO KARLOVASSI • KARLOVASSI

See map pages 114-115; see also photograph page 119

Distance: 15.4km/9.6mi; 3h40min

Grade: easy-moderate. There is some climbing involved, initially to 140m/450ft and similarly again beyond Potami. The final ascent onto the track at the 2h03min-point is a bit of a scramble — avoided in the Alternative walk.

Equipment: stout shoes, sunhat, suncream, sunglasses, long trousers or shorts, long-sleeved shirt, raingear, picnic, water, bathing things

How to get there: 🚐 from Samos to Karlovassi (Timetables 1, 1A); journey time 1h). Daily departures in summer; no Sunday departures in winter.

To return: 🚐 from Karlovassi to Samos (as above; Timetables 1, 1A)

Short walks

1 Karlovassi — Paleo Karlovassi — Ag. Triada — Karlovassi: 5km/3.1mi); 1h10min; easy-moderate; equipment as main walk. Walk only as far as Paleo Karlovassi, visit Ag. Triada (the church on the hill) and, as you come down to the square, look for an old trail on the right which will take you down to the port. Turn right when you reach the coast to head back to Karlovassi.

2 Potami — Tsourlei — Paleo Karlovassi — Karlovassi: 9.4km/5.8mi; 2h30min; easy-moderate; equipment as main walk. Take a taxi to the track leading to the Byzantine church (before Potami beach is reached — on the left after passing the modern church on the right). Follow the main walk from the 1h48min-point.

3 Potami — Tsourlei — Paleo Karlovassi — Karlovassi: 7.9km/4.9mi; 1h50min; easy; equipment as main walk. Take a taxi directly to Potami beach and pick up the *Alternative walk* at the 1h57min-point.

4 Karlovassi — Paleo Karlovassi — Kastro — Potami — Karlovassi: 11km/6.8mi; 2h45min; easy; equipment as main walk. Follow the main walk to Potami, then return along the coastal road from the beach to the port area, where most of the tavernas are located. Keep to the coast road until you reach the sign directing the main flow of traffic inland; follow this to join your outward route to return to the centre of Karlovassi.

Alternative walk (to avoid the scramble at Potami): 16.9km/10.5mi; 3h55min; easy-moderate. Follow the main walk but, at the 1h50min point keep ahead on the road. In 7min start up the track at the far end of Potami bay (1h57min). At a fork 7min later, go back sharp left. Follow this track to Tsourlei, then pick up the main walk again at the 2h16min-point.

Without wishing to do Karlovassi an injustice, it is not the most attractive of towns. It is really a sprawl of three places, New, Middle and Old Karlovassi, and lacks a clear identity. However, it is not without interest, and it probably offers the best shopping on the island (but don't expect tourist shops). In the midst of all this there are oases of charm and character, at Old or 'Paleo' Karlovassi, and Tsourlei.

There are fine views down to the sea from the ruined castle (Kastro), reached in 1h15min.

Bring your swimming costume to enjoy the beach at Potami; it is lovely, and you are sure to be tempted to swim. Have a look at the old Byzantine church which dates back to the 14th century and at the well-concealed old castle *(Kastro)* above it. It took us ages to find the way up to the castle at first, and while we were busy wandering around looking for it, we chanced upon a beautiful spot where the river emerges from a narrow gorge.

Start out from **Karlovassi** centre: head towards the stadium (see plan page 8). Cross the bridge met in **5min**. This is a long bridge over a narrow river and is one of a pair; the other is much nearer the sea. Beyond the bridge, follow the road as it bends around to the right. Then take the first left in **9min**, by a tall palm tree. Looking ahead now, you should soon be able to see Ag. Triada perched high on a hill, making rather a good landmark. Since this is the direction in which we are heading, all you have to do is keep straight on, first as you join another road on a bend and again, in **14min**, when you join a concrete track as the road bends away to the right. In **21min** go left, then right up the cobbled trail which will take you up to **Paleo Karlovassi** in just five minutes. Turn left as you reach the village or first go right, if you want to visit **Ag. Triada** (Picnic 17a) and return to this point to continue. Then head up into the main village square (**28min**). There is just one taverna here, the Taverna Paleo, so if you are only doing Short walk 1, you can take your refreshment in this lovely old *platea* and watch the world go by for a time before heading for Ag. Triada and back downhill.

Onward the hardy. Cross the square and leave by the narrow road to the right. This leads you uphill, to join another road in less than a minute. Turn right and follow this road until it bends away to the left two minutes later. Then continue straight ahead, by joining the track passing to the left side of the chapel. This leads you directly into the countryside. Good views open up almost immediately, particularly of Ag. Triada perched on the hill and of the port down in Karlovassi. As you continue steadily uphill, the views get better until, in **38min**, you can see down over the whole of Karlovassi and the Ambelos Mountains beyond. The track leads through olive groves and sometimes through open pine. Keep right uphill on meeting a crossing track. At present, this track reverts to path at about the **42min**-point, but *be aware* that it may be extended. Herbs like sage and Mediterranean thyme bordering the path contribute to that lovely aromatic smell in the air. There is no shortage of orchids in early spring, and one to look out for here is the naked man orchid, *Orchis italica.* If you inspect any flower in the spike you will notice that it has a man-shaped figure with arms and legs, but it is the appendage between the legs which gives this one its common name.

A clearing with a SHRINE, reached in **42min**, marks the highest point of the walk. (For the curious, a few minutes' diversion is the waymarked path to St. Anthony's cave, which forks off just past the shrine.) As you start into your descent, watch out three minutes later for the path off right which leads within a minute to a secluded CHAPEL and delightful picnic spot (Picnic 17b). Here you can relax under the shade of a plane tree, while you enjoy views down over the olive groves to the sea. Return to the trail and follow it down through woodlands. Keep ahead as you meet a track (**56min**) and stay ahead, ignoring tracks left then right. In **1h**, as the track joins a concrete section of track (where a left turn leads to Leka), turn right. Two minutes later, watch out for the continuation of the trail ahead (by a wall), as the track bends away to the right. In **1h05min** the trail briefly reverts to rough track; continue downhill and around to the left, now back on a narrow trail. You meet the road just two minutes later (**1h07min**). There is a taverna over to the right as you emerge but, if you are more intent on seeing the Byzantine church, turn left and look immediately for the sign directing you up a track on the left. Follow the track, keeping to the right, to reach the CHURCH (Picnic 17c; photograph page 119) in just over two minutes.

The castle *(Kastro)* is set well above the church, and you cannot see it from here, but the way up is through the yard at the side of the church: cross diagonally to the right (through the opening), to join a steeply-rising path. Meet another path within two minutes; turn right to reach the CASTLE two minutes later (**1h15min**). The remains are quite substantial, and the position, too, is impressive — perched on a hillside, with good views out to sea or inland, up a long wooded valley.

Return to the church by the same route. From here you can take a delightful little diversion upriver to visit the glade and the gorge. Turn left as you emerge from the church and follow the waymarked path along the river bank, criss-crossing the river, before finishing up some 12 minutes later at the GORGE (Picnic 17d). Return the same way, passing the church, to reach the road in **1h48min**. *(Short walk 2 begins here.)*

Turn left and, in under two minutes, turn left on a track (**1h50min**). *(But for the Alternative walk, keep ahead on the road here.)* Just before a clearing with a white church (**1h52min**), fork right onto a path which becomes waymarked. As you climb gently, there are views across the valley to the castle visited earlier. Scramble up onto a concrete track (**2h03min**) and turn left. Keep left at the fork seven minutes later, to reach the outskirts of **Tsourlei** in **2h16min**. You pass the lovely old wash-house before reaching the centre of the village.

When you are ready to leave, continue straight through the village along the concrete track. Cross a bridge over the stream (**2h26min**) and fork right immediately, to join a trail. Emerge onto the concreted track again in five minutes and turn right. Just after passing a track off to the right (the route of Walk 19), and then a rubbish tip, take the track to the left (**2h36min**). Head uphill on this track, crossing another track in three minutes, to emerge on the road between a concrete loading bay and block-built bunker (**2h47min**). Turn left and, in two minutes, go left again towards the monastery of Ag. Ioannis. Keep right at a fork, then enjoy some fine views down over Paleo Karlovassi as you descend to **Moni Ag. Ioannis** (**3h01min**). Just before the monastery, fork right down the path to the *platea* in **Paleo Karlovassi**, reached in **3h10min**. To return to **Karlovassi**, retrace your outgoing route (**3h40min**).

18 POTAMI • MIKRO SEITANI • MEGALO SEITANI • DRAKEI

See also photograph page 121   Distance: 10km/6.25mi; 2h40min

Grade: moderate-strenuous. This is an undulating coastal walk which reaches a height of only 375m/1230ft; however, the paths are narrow and sometimes stony. Some people may find sections of the path between Mikro and Megalo Seitani vertiginous.

Equipment: walking boots, sunhat, suncream, sunglasses, long trousers, long-sleeved shirt, cardigan, raingear, picnic, water

How to get there and return: An essential first step when planning this walk is to consider how to get back. Since this is determined by the infrequency of buses back from Drakei, *the return journey details are given first for emphasis. Note that at press date the bus was terminating at Kallithea (7km south of Drakei), due to problems with the unsurfaced track.* **Check the situation before setting out!**

To return: 🚌 from Drakei to Samos (Timetables 3, 3A; journey time 3h). Departures weekdays only. Note: **It is vital to check this departure in advance.**

To get there: 🚌 from Samos to Karlovassi (Timetables 1, 1A; journey time 1h). Daily departures in summer; no Sunday buses in winter. Taxi from Karlovassi to the end of the surfaced road at Potami (4km).

Alternative walks: Both of the bays (Mikro Seitani and Megalo Seitani) are worth visiting. There are no travel problems on these alternatives, since they return from Karlovassi (Timetables 1, 1A).

1 Potami — Mikro Seitani — Potami — Karlovassi: 8.5km/5.3mi; 2h; easy; equipment as above, plus bathing things. Follow the main walk to Mikro Seitani Bay and enjoy this beautiful beach. Return by the same route and, when you reach the coast road at Potami, follow it back to Karlovassi, as described in Short walk 17-4 page 106.

2 Potami — Mikro Seitani — Megalo Seitani — Potami — Karlovassi: 12.6km/7.8mi; 3h; moderate; equipment as above, plus bathing things. Follow the main walk as far as Megalo Seitani Bay, reached in 1h10min, and return the same way. When you reach the coast road at Potami, follow it back to Karlovassi, as described in Short walk 17-4, page 106.

3 Karlovassi — Paleo — Karlovassi — Kastro — Potami — Mikro Seitani — Karlovassi: 15.4km/9.6mi; 4h; moderate; equipment as above, plus bathing things. Add the excursion to Mikro Seitani Bay to Walk 17: start at Karlovassi following Walk 17, page 106. When you get to Potami, continue to the end of the surfaced road and use the notes below as far as Mikro Seitani. Return by the same route to Potami and then follow Walk 17 again to end the walk. See also photographs pages 107, 119.

Note: The main walk is easy to reverse, which is useful for those staying at Ormos Marathokambos or Votsalakia (Kambos). It eliminates the uphill section to Drakei and allows more time to enjoy the beaches on the return. Enquire about boats (in summer) from Karlovassi and Ormos Marathokambos to Ag. Isidoros, a fishing hamlet below Drakei. A 30min walk up the track from there leads directly to Drakei, from where you can use the map to follow the walk in reverse.

Here, in the extreme northwest corner of Samos, is a region of great natural beauty which does not yet bear the imprint of man. If the sheer remoteness of this region (which has no roads and no villages) is not enough for you, then add in two of the most isolated and beautiful bays in the whole of the Aegean and some of the finest coastline on the island. The small and intimate Mikro Seitani Bay is the first one reached; its breathtaking beauty is certain to enthral you. As you leap down on to the sand, it seems for the moment that nowhere else in the world matters. The crystal-clear turquoise sea reveals with clarity the underlying rocks, to remind you that care is needed when bathing here. Megalo Seitani Bay sports a long sweep of sandy beach and is more accessible from the sea than Mikro Seitani. It is a lovely spot to relax and offers the easier bathing of the two bays. Having reached this point, the walk is by no means over: some of the most dramatic scenery lies ahead, as the path takes a slightly higher inland route to head round to Drakei. The Kerkis Mountains crowd in on you at times and give a distinctly alpine feel to the last part of the walk.

Now a word of warning: When you are ready to leave Megalo Seitani for Drakei, make sure that you have **at least 2h** in hand before the bus departure from Drakei. You need time on this last section of the walk not only to enjoy it, but because the narrow and stony paths cannot be taken hastily. The consequences of missing the bus are dire. Drakei has no local taxis, and the nearest ones are located in Marathokambos some 28km/17.5mi away. If you miss the bus, you may be lucky and find some basic accommodation, but the chances are that you will have to walk back to Karlovassi which will make for a very tough day. The bus journey back from Drakei is a long one, but there are some really spectacular views to be enjoyed as you drive over the initially-unsurfaced road of this outback. The mountain scenery of Kerkis on the left vies with the coastal scenery down right. This journey is worth doing in its own right and it does help to make a truly memorable day.

Megalo Seitani

Start out from the end of the surfaced road in **Potami** (Picnic 18a), by joining the ongoing concrete track. Already there is a good viewpoint back over Potami Bay, but this is soon left behind as you head into the pines. Ignore two tracks off right, but go right on a well-waymarked path (**14min**). Almost immediately, the path bends left to traverse the hillside, passing inland of a stone hut. The path now winds downwards through olive groves, giving you glimpses of the beautiful turquoise-blue sea. Enjoying the clean air along these cliffs is a species of the everlasting flower which has large clusters of yellow flowers, making it look very showy. It is not the flowers, but the yellow bracts which have the lasting qualities in these *Helichrysum* species. Ignore the path going off to the left in **26min** (Walk 19

View back to Mikro Seitani Bay, en route to Megalo Seitani

uses this path to divert to Mikro Seitani) and continue along the coast, to reach **Mikro Seitani Bay** (Picnic 18b, photograph page 121) after **36min**.

Some interesting rock formations enclose the beach and shelter this crystal-clear bay, which is reported to be the home of the extremely rare Mediterranean monk seal. When you are ready to move on, head across the beach to leave by the path rising onto the rocks. Even as you leave this lovely bay, you can catch a glimpse of Megalo Seitani ahead, but there's a fair amount of walking still to do, since the path winds around the folds of the hillside before you get there. It is a superb route which takes you through *phrygana* and, as the Kerkis Mountains start to tower higher and closer on the left, the sense of isolation increases. Ignore the path going off to the left in **1h** (the route of Walk 20) and continue ahead in the setting shown opposite, to reach **Megalo Seitani Bay** (**1h10min**). There are some bungalows at the far end of the long beach.

Leave the bay (**1h17min**) by heading for the clear onward path to the left of the beach bungalows. Within five minutes of leaving the beach, you should be passing some caves which appear to be used as stables. At this stage the path is following the coastline, passing through *macchie* and *phrygana*. In **1h36min** stay left when the path divides and starts a gentle climb. Soon viewpoints back down the coast towards Megalo Seitani open up. The surroundings start to change at the higher elevation: vegetation dwindles, and the terrain becomes more rocky until, in **1h57min**, you approach what appears to be an impassable rock barrier. Still climbing, the path heads further inland through a burnt area and into a change of mood. Glimpses of the barren mountains now have a more alpine association and, as you near the highest point of the walk (**2h17min**), there are some glorious views of the peaks ahead.

As the highest point is reached, the path reverts to track. On the far side of the valley, you may be able to see a shrine which stands on the outskirts of Drakei. Follow the track in a U-bend round the valley (there *is* a path which dips down to cross the valley, but it doesn't save much time). In around 16 minutes (two minutes after passing a clear path down to the right and just before the track starts to descend), watch carefully for the path forking up left to **Drakei** (**2h40min**). The bus stops on the far side of the village.

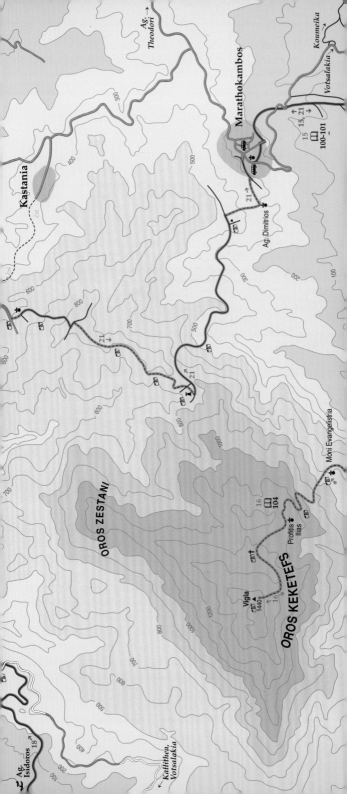

19 KARLOVASSI • PALEO KARLOVASSI • KOSMADEO • (MIKRO SEITANI) • POTAMI • KARLOVASSI

See map pages 114-115   **Distance:** 21.5km/13.4mi; 4h52min

Grade: strenuous. Kosmadeo is at an altitude of 600m/2000ft, and the route up from sea level is steep at times, but at least there is plenty of shade on the way. Some of the paths, tracks and trails used in this walk require careful footwork and cannot be taken hurriedly.

Equipment: walking boots, long trousers, long-sleeved shirt, sunhat, suncream, sunglasses, cardigan, raingear, picnic, water

How to get there: 🚌 from Samos to Karlovassi (Timetables 1, 1A; journey time 1h). Daily departures in summer; no Sunday departures in winter. A taxi from Karlovassi to Paleo Karlovassi to begin, and from the port to Karlovassi at the end, shortens the walk by 5.2km/3.3mi; 1h.
To return: 🚌 from Karlovassi to Samos (Timetables 1, 1A; journey time 1h). Daily departures in summer; no Sunday buses in winter.

Alternative walks: You can choose from a variety of options (all same grade and equipment as the main walk) A few are listed but you can easily devise your own, especially by linking up with Walks 17 or 20.

1 Paleo Karlovassi — (Mikro Seitani) — Potami — port: 11.9km/ 7.4mi; 2h57min. Take a taxi to Paleo Karlovassi and pick up the main walk at the 28min-point. Follow it to the 1h53min-point then skip to the 2h55min-point to walk to the port. Take a taxi back to Karlovassi.

2 Karlovassi — Paleo Karlovassi — Kosmadeo — Paleo Karlovassi — Karlovassi: 20.4km/12.7mi; 4h48min. Follow the main walk to Kosmadeo, then retrace your steps to return.

3 Karlovassi — Paleo Karlovassi — Kosmadeo — (Mikro Seitani) — Potami — Paleo Karlovassi — Karlovassi: 23km/14.3mi; 5h15min. Follow the main walk to the 4h08min-point, then turn right and use the map to return to Karlovassi via Paleo Karlovassi (Walk 17 in reverse).

There is such a fine selection of paths, tracks and trails in this corner of the island that we spent ages finding out where they all led to. Some of the trails, like the one leading towards Kosmadeo, which we use in this walk, are so well built that their construction must have been a task of Herculean proportions. By necessity, these vital communication links had a simple directness, and there was certainly no effort wasted in circumventing steep inclines as you'll find out for yourselves. Having mapped out all these old routes, we had a lot of fun putting them together into interesting walks. So, for this one, once we get you up the hill through the lush and shady vegetation, we bring you down again in the full glare of the sun (although you still have the shade that the olive groves provide, as you descend steeply down the dusty track towards the northwest shore). Once back at sea level, you might just notice the rosemary, a herb sacred to love, friendship and remembrance. It grows in many places, but is always regarded as at its best and most fragrant when growing in dry sandy soil and in the salty atmosphere of the seashore. For this reason it was given the beautiful name 'dew of the sea', *Rosmarinus* in Latin.

The walk starts as you leave the bus in **Karlovassi**. Head first for **Paleo Karlovassi**, following Walk 17 (page 107), until you reach the village square in **28min**. Cross diagonally over the square and leave by ascending the steps alongside the Taverna Paleo. Then continue left along a concrete track. Take the old trail up to the right, reached just three minutes after leaving the square. As you climb through mixed woodland, the vegetation gets greener and taller. In **38min** the trail joins a track near a monastery, where you turn left to head in the direction of Leka. Viewpoints open up across the valley and to the sea; silver-topped olive trees, dark green pines and the massed yellow of Spanish broom combine in an eye-catching splash of colour.

The main road to Leka is reached in **49min**: turn right here but, within two minutes, look for a track on the right which starts between a concrete loading bay and a small building. Keep ahead on this track as it descends, ignoring tracks off to the right. Cross a track (**58min**) and continue for two minutes to a concrete road, where you turn right. In just over one minute (**1h01min**), fork left down a track. Stay on this track, ignoring a track heading up to the left five minutes downhill. You pass a small white church on the left just before reaching a stream (**1h09min**), which may need to be crossed on stepping stones.

Initially, follow the track as it bends right and then left. In one minute, fork right uphill on a path. On reaching a fork (**1h12min**), do not take the waymarked path to the left (it is now blocked), but go right. The path soon swings more to the left, skirting the edge of olive groves, and meets an old cobbled trail four minutes later. At a T-junction (**1h21min**) go left, to continue uphill (a right here leads down to Tsourlei; Walk 20).

Cross the track which cuts across your route (**1h 26min**), to continue up the trail. There are occasional views across to Platanos or up to Kosmadeo, perched high on the hillside. In **1h41min** follow the main trail which swings right (the path straight ahead here is the return route for Walk 20). Continue to climb through the shady pine woods. Suddenly (**1h52min**) you emerge on a track, on a bend: keep ahead here. One minute later (**1h53min**) pass a path down to the right (your return route). Enjoy a little level walking now, with open views over towards Platanos and Ydroussa. Meet a road (**1h57min**) and turn right uphill (left leads to Nikoloudes). Five minutes up the road, fork right on a waymarked path, on a bend. Keep left at a fork, then go sharp left (by a stone ruin). Meeting the road again (**2h05min**), go right. Just over a minute later, keep ahead on a trail, rising up to the road again (by a bend in a descending concrete track; **2h09min**).

Turn right along the road. Almost immediately, on a bend, a track enters from the right (the route of Walk 20). The path up to Kosmadeo continues from the block-built building here, but it is likely to be overgrown: continue up the road, at **2h13min** passing a path coming in from the right (which Walk 20 uses to divert to Kosmadeo). As the road sweeps left (**2h15min**), keep ahead on a concrete path. It immediately swings left as a continuation of the old trail. Join the road again, five minutes later, below Kosmadeo, and follow it round to the right. You pass the start of Walk 21 (the concrete road off to the right) just before reaching the village square (**2h 24min**). There is a *kafeneion* here, and more along the street through the village. **Kosmadeo** is an interesting village to explore, and there are good views from the start of Walk 21 and from the far end of the village. An old trail descends to Kastania from the far end of the village; blocked by forest fires in 2000, it is once again viable (see 'Stop Press', page 135).

When you have finished exploring Kosmadeo, retrace your steps to the track below the Nikoloudes-Kosmadeo road and follow it to the path first passed at the 1h53min-point (**2h55min**). Turn left down this waymarked path (it was on your right on your ascent). In under three minutes the path ahead may be blocked by trees, so follow a path down left into an olive grove and leave it via a track on the right. Turn right on meeting a crossing track, to reach the white church of saints Constantine and Eleni, up left, in five minutes. Continue down the track, but look for the waymarked path down left just after rounding the next bend. You will come back to the track just before it ends (**3h08min**): turn left. Almost immediately, the path continues off the end of the track. (*But note that further bulldozing could extend this track.*) Stay with the waymarked path as it winds down the hillside. Megalo Seitani comes into view with its red-roofed summer houses as you approach the shore. Near the bottom of the descent, the path bends round to the right and, shortly afterwards (**3h35min**), you reach a junction. Our route is ahead, but if you wish to divert to Mikro Seitani, go down left and, when you come to a T-junction in eight minutes, turn left. After visiting the bay, return the same way, but keep left past your descent route, rejoining the main walk track about 10 minutes short of Potami.

This lovely waymarked path traverses the hillside towards Potami for eight minutes, before emerging on a track (**3h47min**). Keep ahead, and keep left at the fork a minute later. Pass the path off left to Mikro Seitani and eight minutes later come to a fork. A right turn here leads to Tsourlei; fork left, down to **Potami** (**4h**).

The return to Karlovassi along the coastal road takes a little over 50 minutes. Continue along the road round the bay, passing the track off right to the Byzantine church shown below and, a minute later (**4h08min**), the start of the path over to Paleo Karlovassi. *(Turn right here for Alternative walk 3.)* Keeping ahead along the road brings you down into the port area, where most of the tavernas are located. Stay with the coast road until you reach the sign which directs the main flow of traffic inland: follow this to return to the inland bridge and back to the bus station at **Karlovassi** (**4h52min**).

Picnic 17c: the lovely setting of the Byzantine church behind Potami. Just a few minutes above it lies a well-concealed old castle (photograph page 107). To get there, cross the yard behind the church (as you see it here) and take the path leading uphill.

20 POTAMI • MIKRO SEITANI • (KOSMADEO) NIKOLOUDES • TSOURLEI • PALEO KARLOVASSI • KARLOVASSI

See map pages 114-115; see also photograph page 112

Distance: 18km/11.2mi; 4h34min

Grade: moderate-strenuous. The hard work is confined to an ascent from sea level up to 475m/1560ft; the rest of the walk is downhill.

Equipment: walking boots, long trousers, long-sleeved shirt, sunhat, suncream, sunglasses, raingear, picnic, water, bathing things

How to get there: 🚌 from Samos to Karlovassi (Timetables 1, 1A; journey time 1h). Daily departures in summer; no Sunday buses in winter. Taxi from Karlovassi to the end of the surfaced road at Potami (5.2km).

To return: 🚐 from Karlovassi to Samos (Timetables 1, 1A; journey time 1h). Daily departures in summer; no Sunday buses in winter.

It would pay to start this walk as early in the day as possible, especially during the high season, since the uphill section is rather exposed and is best avoided in the full heat of the sun. As always, the climb is worthwhile when you actually arrive at the top. Two old villages lie en route, although you may only have time to see one of them: Nikoloudes. The other — Kosmadeo — if added to this walk, requires an extra 30 minutes' walking, plus sightseeing time. (Kosmadeo features in Walks 19 and 21, so if you plan to do one of those walks, miss it out on this occasion.) One of the fascinations of these isolated villages is the insight gained into the old lifestyles. Some of the old stone-built ovens (see page 88) are still to be seen in the gardens, and indeed some of them are still in use, particularly at Eastertime. In the old days these ovens, often communal, were fired up with wooden logs usually once a week. Pine wood was used mostly, even if it meant lopping off the lower branches of the trees around the village — and the evidence is still to be seen. Bread was then baked for the whole week, with all the villagers awaiting their turn. As one of the old villagers told us, newly-baked bread was not eaten until the previous week's bake had been consumed. As a consequence, some of the older folk actually prefer stale bread and, even today, bread bought fresh from the baker is stored to 'maturity'.

Start the walk as you leave the taxi at the end of the surfaced road in **Potami**: use the notes for Walk 18 (see page 112). Once you are beyond **Mikro Seitani Bay** and just before reaching Megalo Seitani Bay, look for a path on the left (**1h**), which starts you on the uphill section. The route climbs first towards the left through woods and olive groves, but soon leaves any shade behind as it swings right into more open terrain ... and climbs more steeply. When the path emerges on a track (**1h28min**), follow the track uphill for less than three minutes (past a farm building and then a water tank, both on the right), to locate your ongoing path also on the right.

Mikro Seitani: this unbelievably beautiful bay is visited on both Walks 18 and 20. Megalo Seitani is the beach in the middle distance.

Keep straight ahead on the path/trail, as it crosses the same track shortly afterwards. Turn left at **1h40min**, where the path joins a concrete section of a track, and continue uphill, now climbing less steeply. Ignore a track off to the left, but keep left when another track joins from the right (**1h51min**); continue ahead here. A strong path forks up to the right at **2h12min***, stay ahead on the track to meet the Kosmadeo road on a bend three minutes later (**2h15min**). Head left for Nikoloudes. Almost immediately, take a path off left (off the corner of a concrete track). You rejoin the road in three minutes and, a minute later, pick up a further section of path cutting a loop off the road. When you again meet the road, turn left to head down to Nikoloudes, ignoring a track off left (which Walk 19 ascends from Tsourlei).

Nikoloudes is reached at **2h36min**. There is a huge plane tree here, said to be the biggest and oldest on Samos, and an old wash-house on the left. Our walk continues along the path immediately before the plane tree. Follow the path down through open cultivated fields, towards the pine woods until, at **2h46min**, you join an old trail (the route of Walk 19), just on a bend. Here go straight ahead downhill, taking full advantage of the shade provided by the leafy surrounds. Keep ahead as a track crosses the trail (**3h**). Ignore the trail off to the right at **3h05min** (the ascent route of Walk 19), and continue downwards alongside the water channel. You reach **Tsourlei** just seven minutes later (**3h12min**). The village has no taverna, but at least there is drinking water on tap.

At the junction reached almost immediately, turn right to continue but, if you wish to see the church of Ag. Pandeleimon and the old wash-house, then wander off to the left. The church is well known on the island, and its name is often used to refer to the village. When you are ready to leave, follow the notes for Walk 17 from the 2h16min-point (page 109), to walk from this village back to the bus stop in **Karlovassi** (**4h34min**).

*To divert to Kosmadeo, go up this path. In three minutes you join Walk 19 at the 2h13min-point; see page 118 to continue up to the village. Return the same way, but continue down the road — first passing the path where you joined the road and then, a few minutes later, a track descending from the left. This is the track followed in the main walk; pick up the main walk again at the 2h15min point.

21 KOSMADEO TO MARATHOKAMBOS

See map pages 114-115

Distance: 10km/6.2mi; 2h30min

Grade: moderate, but only suitable for experienced walkers — route-finding can be difficult on the path between the 34min- and 1h06min-points, and there is some danger of vertigo along this section as well.

Equipment: walking boots, long trousers, long-sleeved shirt, sunhat, suncream, sunglasses, raingear, picnic, water

How to get there: 🚍 from Samos to Karlovassi (Timetables 1, 1A; journey time 1h). Daily departures in summer; no Sunday buses in winter. Taxi from Karlovassi to Kosmadeo (30min).

To return: 🚍 from Marathokambos to Samos (Timetable 3, 3A; journey time 1h30min). Or taxi from Marathokambos to Karlovassi (20min), then bus to Samos (Timetables 1,1A; journey time 1h). Daily departures in summer; no Sunday buses in winter.

One of the fascinating aspects of Samos is the change in vegetation in the various parts of the island. Over in the east, the typical dry Mediterranean *macchie* and *phrygana* grow in abundance. But even there you will notice differences between the northeast and southeast, arising from micro-climatic variations (chiefly throughout the winter months). Thus you will find different plant species or simply different flowering times, particularly in the earlier spring months. The southern part of the island is the hottest and driest region, where commercial citrus farms are located at low altitudes, typically around Mili. Mixed

Just after leaving Kosmadeo, your view stretches down right over a cultivated valley and out to sea.

deciduous forests cloak the flanks of the Ambelos range, and plane trees dominate by rivers and streams. Some of the loveliest valleys on the island are found here. Finally, the northwest corner, in the shadow of the giant Kerkis Mountain range, is the most luxuriant part of all. To walk in this area is to enjoy some of the most dramatic scenery on the island, and that's where we are taking you on this walk. You can see for yourselves the change in the vegetation as you head south, and the transformation is complete before Marathokambos is reached.

Alight from the taxi at the entrance to **Kosmadeo**. **Start the walk** by heading back downhill for half a minute, then keep ahead to the left on a concrete road which contours the cultivated valley down to the right, with wide views towards the coast. As the road completes a U around the valley and starts to rise, Kosmadeo is seen over to the right, perched on a spur. In around **14min**, look for a stony path (almost like a rough stream bed) off to the left. This takes you past a pool of water on the left and immediately becomes a clear, waymarked path as it climbs to the right. Rise up to where there is a small church over to the left and head towards it, passing through a gap in the low wall (**20min**).

Walk to the right of the church and, on the far side,

124

continue in almost the same direction on a track which climbs almost due south. This track rises up along a ridge, to reach a great viewpoint over the Kerkis valley 10 minutes later. In **31min** you reach a vineyard: skirt round it to the right. On coming to a crossing track in just over two minutes, turn left. Then, as you round the first bend (**34min**), take a path off to the right. There are occasional waymarks but, basically, the path is following the right-hand side of the ridge, just below the summit. In the first few minutes, the path can be a little vague as it wanders briefly to the top of the ridge and then back again. Just remember to stay roughly on the same contour along the right-hand side of the ridge, without deviating too much to the left or right.

Fallen trees in an area of woodland (**41min**) may cause small diversions during the next five minutes, especially in spring after the winter rains. Do not be tempted to descend too far, and always relocate your path. The path then runs along a woodland ledge before emerging out in the open, to cross a scree (**47min**). Along here the views are fantastic, as you can see in the photograph above. Set in this wild and hostile grandeur, the monastery of Ag. Ioannis lies cradled in the bottom of the valley, while the ridge of Kerkis, across the valley, runs south to the highest summit on the island — Vigla (Walk 16). Vertigo might be a problem along the next section, as the path lies close to the edge. At around **55min**, where the path is vague, keep more or less on the same level, and ignore paths forking up left to the top of the ridge in the next three minutes. In **1h03min** you rise up to cross the saddle of a spur which juts out into the valley — a good vantage point and picnic spot.

There is an element of surprise as the path suddenly emerges out in the open (**1h06min**), with more panoramic views. The way now lies across a wide saddle in the direction of a monument seen near a track. Continue diagonally down to the left, to cross a minor track and reach the monument. The position of the monument on the saddle is a good landmark between the two valleys. Join the nearby major track (**1h10min**) and turn left towards Marathokambos.

As you start into a winding descent from the saddle, your onward track can be clearly seen, ribboning ahead along the contours of the hill to the left. The barren terrain contrasts sharply with the more lush vegetation in the first part of the walk. Marathokambos and Ormos Marathokambos come into view as you round a bend (**1h55min**). Look now for a blue-domed church down to the right, your next landfall. Ignore a track down to the right in two minutes but, just after a ruined stone house (also down on the right; **2h**), take the stony path heading sharply back to the right. It takes you to the blue-domed church of **Ag. Dimitrios** (**2h12min**), a good spot to rest.

Leave the church by heading down the concrete path. This becomes a stony path and leads to a crossing track, where you turn left. In a few minutes, take the concreted right fork, to head down into **Marathokambos**. Stay right then go right and left, just before a

Approaching the saddle crossed some 1h03min into the walk

Old Route from Ormos Marathokambos to Marathokambos

(2.4km/1.5mi; 45min; easy; map pages 100-101)

This walk can be used as an extension to Walks 15 and 21, or as a short walk in its own right.

From the harbour at **Ormos Marathokambos** follow the road inland, to the right. Cross the road reached in under two minutes and keep heading uphill, to the left of the church. In **4min**, cross the road again and continue up a stony track opposite. Keep ahead as a track forks off right. After passing some neglected greenhouses on the right, reach a further fork (**13min**). Go left and ignore tracks coming in from the left (take care if you are doing the walk in reverse, as the track passed in **19min** into the ascent appears to be the more major track on the descent). Meet the road (**23min**) and cross it, joining a short section of cobbled trail. Two minutes later, cross the road slightly to the right, and pick up a short section of path which cuts a further loop off the road.

Cross the road for a final time to enter the now-concreted trail (**25min**) which leads up to Marathokambos. Follow the old route past a white church on the left. As the trail bends left (**32min**), pass a shrine/fountain on the right and the remains of an old aqueduct. On the outskirts of **Marathokambos** (**36min**) the trail becomes a narrow street with a central channel. Continue up this street, with a gully over to the left, to pass the old and interesting church of Ag. Varvara (St Barbara), dating from 1795. Keep following the street with the channel as it bends left to cross the now-narrow gully near a shop. (It is easy to become disorientated amongst the narrow streets of the town.) The street passes below the main church up on the right, to emerge opposite the school and playground. Turn right and follow the road uphill, passing the entrance to the main church on the right. You come into the *platea*, where there are tavernas and taxis. The bus stops on the main road, a short walk beyond the platea, to the left.

To do the walk in reverse (descending from Marathokambos), head down the road from the *platea,* to the right of the main church. Opposite the school and playground, turn left into a street with a central channel. Stay with this street with the channel as it skirts below the village and bends right across a gully, passes Ag. Varvara and then heads left into a concreted trail. Now refer to the map on pages 100-181 to complete the descent; once clear of Marathokambos, the way is quite straightforward.

gully. Head round to the right before reaching a house with an arch, then go down the steps to the right of the church, to the main road There is a café here, and the bus for Samos stops across the road from it (**2h30min**).

If you would like to continue down to Ormos Marathokambos, turn right down the main road and locate the church in the main square on the left in a couple of minutes. Then see the last paragraph in the box above.

BUS TIMETABLES

Our long walks are based on the frequency of the winter timetables, denoted below by the suffix A, so that they can be done all the year round. In summer there are many more buses running, which give more flexibility in the travel times and allow one or two extra short walks to be included. Below is a list of destinations covered in the timetables. The timetables themselves are found on pages 129 to 132. Numbers following place names below refer to the *timetable* numbers.

The period of the summer timetable is from around mid-June to mid-September. The winter timetable, denoted by the suffix 'A', applies at all other times.

See also the important 'Hints on using the local bus service' below.

Ag. Dimitrios: 1, 1A
Ag. Konstantinos: 1, 1A
Avlakia: 1, 1A
Chora: 2, 4, 4A
Drakei: 3, 3A
Ireon: 7, 7A
Kambos 1, 1A
Karlovassi: 1, 1A, 2, 3, 3A, 8, 9
Kastania: 9
Kokkari: 1, 1A
Kosmadeo: 9
Koumaradei: 2
Leka: 9
Marathokambos: 3, 3A

Mavratzei Junction: 2
Mesokambos: 4, 4A
Mytilini: 4, 4A
Pagondas: 7, 7A
Platanakia: 1, 1A
Platanos Crossroads: 2
Psili Ammos: 5
Pyrgos: 2
Pythagorion: 2, 4, 4A
Samos town: 1, 1 A, 2, 3, 3A, 4, 4A, 5, 6, 7, 7A
Votsalakia: 3, 3A
Vourliotes Junction: 1, 1A, 6
Ydroussa 8, 8A

Hints on using the local bus service

Please do not rely *solely* on the timetables shown on the following pages; be prepared to check your bus departure and return times before setting out. Timetables change basically twice a year, and printed copies are often available at the bus station and the main tourist information office in Samos town; these are more reliable than the postings on some tourist office walls.

Buses are numbered, but check the destination shown on the front and, if you are at all uncertain, do check with the conductor as you board the bus.

The winter period for buses extends for most of the year, from September right through until June. Buses released from school duties are used to improve the summer service, so often there is no sharp cut-off point, and services are simply increased steadily throughout May and June as and when buses become available.

One point worth remembering: buses often stop on request virtually anywhere so, if you are caught between bus stops, don't hesitate to flag the bus down but, equally, don't rely on it!

1 SAMOS to KARLOVASSI (via the coast road and
Ag. Konstantinos)
SUMMER; weekdays only

Samos	08.30	11.00	12.20	14.00	15.00	
	17.00	20.00				
Kokkari	08.45	11.15	12.35	14.15	15.15	
	17.15	20.15				
Avlakia	08.55	11.25	12.45	14.25	15.25	
	17.25	20.25				
Vourliotes (J)	08.57	11.27	12.47	14.27	15.27	
	17.27	20.27				
Platanakia	09.00	11.30	12.50	14.30	15.30	
	17.30	20.30				
Ag.Konstantinos	09.02	11.32	12.52	14.32	15.32	
	17.32	20.32				
Ag.Dimitrios	09.17	11.47	13.07	14.47	15.47	
	17.47	20.37				
Karlovassi	09.25	11.55	13.15	14.55	15.55	
	17.55	20.55				

Saturdays:
Departure times from Samos: 08.30; 11.00; 14.00; 17.00; 12.00
Sundays:
Departure times from Samos: 08.30; 14.00; 17.00; 19.00
NB: *There are many extra buses from Samos to Tsamadou Beach via Kokkari and return, in addition to the above timetable, every day of the week.*

KARLOVASSI to SAMOS (via the coast road and Ag. Konstantinos)
SUMMER; weekdays

Karlovassi	07.00	08.15	09.30	12.30	14.30	
	16.45	18.00				
Ag.Dimitrios	07.08	08.23	09.38	12.38	14.38	
	16.53	18.08				
Ag.Konstantinos	07.23	08.38	09.53	12.53	14.53	
	17.08	18.23				
Platanakia	07.25	08.40	09.55	12.55	14.55	
	17.10	18.25				
Vourliotes (J)	07.28	08.43	09.58	12.58	14.58	
	17.13	18.28				
Avlakia	07.30	08.45	10.00	13.00	15.00	
	17.15	18.30				
Kokkari	07.40	08.55	10.10	13.10	15.10	
	17.25	18.40				
Samos	07.55	09.10	10.25	13.25	15.25	
	17.40	18.55				

Saturdays:
Departure times from Karlovassi: 07.15; 09.30; 12.30; 14.30; 18.00
Sundays:
Departure times from Karlovassi: 09.30; 12.30; 15.00; 18.00

Continues overleaf (Timetable 1A)

J = road junction

1A SAMOS to KARLOVASSI (via the coast road and Ag. Konstantinos)
WINTER; weekdays

Samos	08.30	11.00	12.20	14.30	15.00	17.00
Kokkari	08.45	11.15	12.35	14.45	15.15	17.15
Avlakia	08.55	11.25	12.45	14.55	16.25	17.25
Vourliotes (J)	08.57	11.27	12.47	14.57	16.27	17.27
Platanakia	09.00	11.30	12.50	15.00	16.30	17.30
Ag.Konstantinos	09.02	11.32	12.52	15.02	16.32	17.32
Ag.Dimitrios	09.17	11.47	13.07	15.17	16.47	17.47
Karlovassi	09.25	11.55	13.15	15.25	16.55	17.55

NB: *There are one or two additional buses that run only as far as Kokkari.*
Saturdays:
Departure times from Samos: 08.30; 14.00; 17.00
Sundays:
No buses

KARLOVASSI to SAMOS (via the coast road and Ag. Konstantinos)
WINTER; weekdays

Karlovassi	07.00	08.15	09.30	12.30	14.20	16.45
Ag.Dimitrios	07.08	08.38	09.08	12.08	14.28	16.53
Ag.Konstantinos	07.23	08.53	09.53	12.23	14.43	17.08
Platanakia	07.25	08.55	09.55	12.25	14.45	17.10
Vourliotes (J)	07.28	08.58	09.58	12.28	14.48	17.13
Avlakia	07.30	09.00	10.00	12.30	14.50	17.15
Kokkari	07.40	09.10	10.10	12.40	15.00	17.25
Samos	07.55	09.25	10.25	12.55	15.15	17.45

Saturdays:
Departure times from Karlovassi: 09.30; 12.30; 15.00
Sundays:
No buses

2 SAMOS to KARLOVASSI (inland via Pyrgos)
ALL YEAR ROUND; **weekdays (Mon-Fri) only**

Samos	14.00
Pythagorion	14.20
Chora	14.28
Mavratzei (J)	14.34
Koumaradeoi	14.46
Pyrgos	15.00
Platanos (J)	15.25
Karlovassi	15.40

KARLOVASSI to SAMOS (inland via Pyrgos)
ALL YEAR ROUND; **weekdays (Mon-Fri) only**

Karlovassi	06.15
Platanos (J)	06.30
Pyrgos	06.55
Koumaradeoi	07.09
Mavratzei (J)	07.19
Chora	07.27
Pythagorion	07.35
Samos	07.55

J = road junction

3 SAMOS—KARLOVASSI—VOTSALAKIA—DRAKEI
Note: Until long-delayed road repairs are undertaken, this bus will terminate/begin from Drakei; check in advance!
SUMMER; **Monday, Wednesday and Friday only**

Samos	12.20
Karlovassi	13.20
Marathokambos	13.45
Votsalakia	14.05
Kallithea	14.40
Drakei	*see above*

DRAKEI—VOTSALAKIA—KARLOVASSI—SAMOS
SUMMER; **Monday, Wednesday and Friday only**

Drakei	*see above*
Kallithea	~~00.00~~ I 14.40
Votsalakia	07.10 I 15.15
Marathokambos	07.30 I 15.35
Karlovassi	07.55 I 16.00
Samos	09.05 I 17.30

Saturdays:
~~00.00~~ No service

3A SAMOS—MARATHOKAMBOS / *MARATHOKAMBOS—SAMOS*
WINTER; **Monday, Wednesday and Friday only**
Just one bus from Samos at 12.20, currently running only as far as Votsalakia. Returns from Votsalakia at 15.15. There is no service on Saturdays or Sundays.

4 SAMOS—PYTHAGORION—MYTILINI—SAMOS
SUMMER; weekdays
Samos to Pythagorion (direct): 08.00; 09.30; 11.00; 12.15; 12.45; 14.00; 16.00; 17.00; 18.00
Samos to Pythagorion (via Mytilini): 09.45
Samos to Mytilini: 08.00; 09.45; 11.00; 12.45; 17.00 (all via Pythagorion, except for the bus at 09.45)
Saturdays:
Samos to Pythagorion (direct): 08.00; 09.30; 11.00; 12.00; 12.45; 14.00; 16.00; 17.00; 19.00
Samos to Mytilini (via Pythagorion): 08.00; 11.00; 12.45; 17.00
Sundays:
Samos to Pythagorion: 11.00; 14.00; 16.00

PYTHAGORION—MYTILINI—SAMOS
SUMMER; weekdays
Pythagorion to Samos: 07.25; 08.00; 10.15; 12.55; 15.15; 16.20; 18.40
Mytilini to Samos: 08.30; 11.30; 13.15; 17.30
Saturdays
Pythagorion to Samos: 10.10; 12.15; 14.45; 16.15; 17.15
Chora—Mytilini—Samos: 08.25; 11.25; 13.10; 17.25
Sundays
Pythagorion to Samos: 11.15; 14.15; 16.15

Continues overleaf (Timetable 4A)

4A SAMOS—PYTHAGORION—MYTILINI—SAMOS
WINTER; weekdays
Samos to Pythagorion (direct): 06.10; 08.00; 11.00; 12.15; 12.45;
14.00; 17.00
Samos to Pythagorion (via Mytilini): 08.00; 09.45
Samos to Mytilini: 08.00; 09.45; 11.00; 12.45; 17.00 (all via
Pythagorion except for the buses at 08.00 and 09.45)
Saturdays:
Samos to Pythagorion: 07.30; 11.00; 14.00; 16.00 (all call at
Mytilini except for the bus at 14.00)
Sundays: No service

PYTHAGORION—MYTILINI—SAMOS
Pythagorion to Samos (direct): 07.30; 08.00; 10.20; 15.15
Pythagorion to Samos (via Mytilini): 11.20; 13.05; 17.20
Chora—Mytilini—Samos: 07.50; 08.20; 10.10; 11.25; 13.10;
17.25
Saturdays:
Pythagorion to Samos: 07.50; 11.20; 14.20; 16.20 (all via Mytilini
except for the bus at 14.20)
Sundays: No service

5 SAMOS—PSILI AMMOS—SAMOS
SUMMER only; weekdays

Samos	09.30 I	12.45 I	16.00
Psili Ammos	09.50 I	13.05 I	16.20
Samos	10.10 I	13.15 I	16.40

6 SAMOS to VOURLIOTES
*SUMMER; **Mondays, Wednesdays and Fridays only***
Departs Samos 14.00; returns from Vourliotes 14.45

7 SAMOS—IREON—(PAGONDAS)—SAMOS
SUMMER; weekdays

Samos to Ireon:	06.10 I	09.30 I	12.15 I	14.00 I	18.00
Ireon to Samos:	07.20 I	10.00 I	12.45 I	15.05 I	18.30

The buses departing Samos at 06.10 and 14.00 go to Pagondas via
Mili. Return from Pagondas via Mili at 07.00 and 14.50.
Saturdays

Samos to Ireon:	09.30 I	14.00
Ireon to Samos:	10.00 I	14.30

Sundays: no service

7A IREON—SAMOS
*WINTER; **Mondays, Wednesdays and Fridays only***
Samos to Pagondas via Ireon and Mili: 06.10; 14.00
Pagondas via Mili and Ireon to Samos: 07.10; 14.50
Saturdays and Sundays: no service

8 KARLOVASSI—YDROUSSA—KARLOVASSI
*SUMMER; **Tuesdays only***
Departs Karlovassi at 07.45 and 12.30
Returns from Ydroussa at 08.10 and 12.55

8A KARLOVASSI—YDROUSSA
WINTER: no service

● Index

Geographical entries only are included in this index. For other entries, see Contents, page 3. A page number in *italic type* indicates a map reference; a page number in **bold type** indicates a photograph or drawing. Both of these may be in addition to a text reference on the same page. '*TM*' refers to the large-scale walking map on the reverse of the touring map. Pronunciation hints follow place names. Bus timetables are given on pages 128 to 132.

133